Poland-Mexico: Towards a Strategic Partnership

STUDIES IN POLITICS, SECURITY AND SOCIETY

Edited by Stanisław Sulowski
Faculty of Political Science and International Studies
University of Warsaw

VOLUME 28

PETER LANG

Anita Oberda-Monkiewicz

Poland-Mexico: Towards a Strategic Partnership

PETER LANG

Bibliographic Information published by the Deutsche Nationalbibliothek
The Deutsche Nationalbibliothek lists this publication in
the Deutsche Nationalbibliografie; detailed bibliographic
data is available in the internet at http://dnb.d-nb.de.

Library of Congress Cataloging-in-Publication Data
A CIP catalog record for this book has been applied for
at the Library of Congress.

This publication has been financially supported by the University of
Warsaw

Printed by CPI books GmbH, Leck

ISSN 2199-028X
ISBN 978-3-631-81390-4 (Print)
E-ISBN 978-3-631-81538-0 (E-PDF)
E-ISBN 978-3-631-81539-7 (EPUB)
E-ISBN 978-3-631-81540-3 (MOBI)
DOI 10.3726/b16671

© Peter Lang GmbH
Internationaler Verlag der Wissenschaften
Berlin 2020
All rights reserved.

Peter Lang – Berlin · Bern · Bruxelles · New York ·
Oxford · Warszawa · Wien

This publication has been peer reviewed.

www.peterlang.com

Contents

Introduction

It might seem that there are few countries whose perceptions of international reality could be more different than Poland and Mexico. In fact, however, more unites them than divides them. This book's title, *"Poland-Mexico: Towards a Strategic Partnership"*, represents not just a fond wish, but a reflection of Mexico's real and growing importance in Polish foreign policy as a valuable ally and economic partner. Indeed, the long process of strengthening bilateral relations is to culminate in a strategic partnership, announced by the Polish President Andrzej Duda during a visit to Mexico in 2017. Making this a reality is a big challenge for both states, which have traditionally focused on other geographical areas; yet it may bring long-term mutual benefits that will make it possible for them to diversify their partnerships, strengthen their positions in other regions of the globe, and above all, significantly expand their activities internationally.

However, to fully understand Mexico's place in Polish foreign policy, it is worth examining the broader context of Poland's relations with all of Latin America and the Caribbean. Due to, among other factors, its geographical remoteness, this region has never been the main point of reference for Poland, and contacts between the two have been conditioned by their different historical experience and, during the Cold War, their affiliation with opposing spheres of influence. Their political differences, as well as their similar structures of trade exchange, were not conducive to a deepening of relations. Direct contacts were developed, though, including through the growing group of Polish emigrants in Latin America and the Caribbean.

Traditionally, Poland's foreign policy priorities have been Europe and Poland's immediate vicinity, with the result that areas outside Europe, including Latin America and the Caribbean, have not been figured so strongly. However, the process of globalisation has meant that the world is paying more and more attention to developing countries, which, through political alliances and encouraging economic results, are becoming increasingly important players on the international stage. Poland is also aware of the need to intensify its relations with non-European countries. This was given a strong impulse when Poland acceded to the European Union, since accession entailed an obligation to take a more active role with regard to Latin America and the Caribbean, and also provided access to EU mechanisms for cooperating with the region.

The text which follows aims to show the evolution of Poland's foreign policy towards Latin America, and the main determinants and programmatic assumptions thereof. Relations with Latin America, including Mexico, have developed steadily, but slowly, and their potential has not yet been fully taken advantage of, despite the attempts that have been made.

The concept of "strategic partnership" is not clearly defined. It can be described as "a relationship between countries that exceeds the level of their international cooperation with other countries" (Stemplowski 2001: 141). The objectives of the strategic partnership are "in addition to ensuring security (political, military, energy and so on), first of all to obtain the most favourable position internationally. Using the language of game theory, this tends to be defined as the pursuit of maximising the benefits and minimizing losses" (Bałon 2001: 414). The partners therefore are linked by strategic objectives and will cooperate in their implementation and "if a strategic partnership is not to be merely an empty word, it must also assume that neither party will take action that could adversely affect the security of the other state or hinder the implementation of its objectives" (Burant 2000: 9–10). At the core of the strategic partnership, there is certainly a close cooperation between the parties, both on a bilateral level and in multilateral relations. A common goal, often strictly defined, is the driving force behind cooperation. What is the most important, a real "strategic partnership" cannot be based solely on political declarations and it is necessary to fill it with meaning.

Currently, the term "strategic partnership" is, however, subject to some devaluation, mainly due to the increasingly frequent practice of using it for purely political purposes and limiting to courtesy visits and declarations. The idea of a strategic partnership in a formal and substantive sense thus should be distinguished. In the formal sense, "a strategic partnership is a relationship between entities that is just called formal by the representatives of these entities" (Bałon 2001: 412–413). These include statements made on the occasion of official meetings, interviews, etc. Such declarations undoubtedly act as a gesture of goodwill and diplomatic coincidence, but in most cases remain only on paper and do not substantially change the relationship between states. The strategic partnership in the substantive sense is a system of relations between certain entities which, irrespective of the terms used, fulfils certain conditions like f.i. mutual preference and intensification of contacts, much further than relations with other countries; institutionalising mutual links; and the community of strategic objectives within security and foreign policy, or the equitable position of the parties (Osińska 2007: 28).

The purpose of the following text is to discuss bilateral relations between Poland and Mexico, including both political, economic and cultural perspectives, as well as the role of Polish migration to Mexico. The main research questions are: How historically the determinants of bilateral relations have been formed?

What variables shape them to a decisive extent? Is the strategic partnership declared by both parties substantive, or is it merely a rhetorical gesture?

Analysing Polish-Mexican relations one can see that in the past a strategic partnership between states, as a result of geographic distance, complicated historical experiences, differences in political systems, or belonging to different spheres of influence, in practice could not exist. It was not until the end of the 20th century and the political and economic changes in both countries that led to gradual rapprochement and made both states to form a joint declaration, "towards a strategic partnership between Poland and Mexico" in 2017. However, although the strategic partnership between the two countries was officially initiated, it is not yet institutionalized and needs to be filled with concrete content. In the future, therefore, with the goodwill and commitment of both parties, it can be strengthened and institutionalized in a way that can bring mutual benefits on many levels for both nations.

Historical outline of Poland's relations with Latin America

Relations between Poland and the region of Latin America and the Caribbean have been largely determined by their geographical remoteness from each other and historical factors. Poland never engaged in territorial expansion outside Europe, while its relative stability and religious tolerance did not provoke large waves of emigration to the New World. At the time when the Latin American states were fighting for their independence at the beginning of the 19th century, Poland did not exist as a sovereign state, since from 1772 to 1795 it had been gradually partitioned among three neighbouring states – Russia, Austria, and Prussia. This, of course, meant that no diplomatic or trade relations with Poland could be established. Numerous Polish officers, especially from Napoleon's armies, did take part in the wars for independence fought in the Americas, as did scientists and engineers. In many cases, banished by fate to the New World, they contributed to the science and culture of the young Latin American countries, but these were individual contacts, and Polish issues were largely perceived as internal problems of the partitioning states (Spyra 2006: 383).

Latin America became a destination of choice for Polish emigrants, especially economic emigrants, beginning in the second half of the 19th century. They headed mainly to South America, where it was easy to obtain land. Often treated as citizens of the partitioning states, they found it difficult to assimilate, although the Polish émigré community in Mexico formed a kind of exception. It was largely composed of people of Jewish descent, who quite quickly integrated with the Mexican society.

When Poland regained its independence in 1918 after 123 years of being partitioned, it got an opportunity to redefine its foreign policy and create the foundations for official cooperation with Latin America. Yet, maintaining relations with the region would draw attention away from Poland's efforts to finally settle its own borders, preserve its hard-won independence, and rebuild its shattered economy. As Jarosław Spyra has written, "Poland – both after regaining independence in 1918 and during the period of the Polish People's Republic, a state of limited sovereignty – never formed a clear, cohesive and consistent policy towards Latin America. The region was not a priority and, in terms of Polish interests, was completely peripheral". The standard model of relations with the countries of Latin America posited that these are distant, exotic countries from which little can be gained apart from specific cultural achievements and raw materials. Cultural cooperation involved literature and music, while trade exchange – quite substantial in certain years, especially after World War II – was limited mainly to commodities and goods involving little processing (Spyra 2006: 384).

As a result, during the interbellum period, Poland's relations with the countries of Latin America and the Caribbean were very much limited in scope and, apart from issues of migration, Poland showed little interest in the region. During World War II, Poland attempted to recruit Poles living in Latin America for the Polish armed forces, though to little effect. Latin America did become a destination, though, for a wave of Polish war refugees, and after 1945 for political refugees as well who were unwilling or unable to return home after the war for fear they would face repressions at the hands of the now communist state.

Evolution of Latin American policy after 1945

After the end of the World War II, Poland became part of the Soviet bloc, which discouraged most Latin American countries from maintaining deep relations with it. Direct contacts became infrequent and solely formal. The states of Latin America, situated within the sphere of influence of the United States of America (USA), were mostly governed by right-wing regimes antagonistic towards communism, which prevented mutual understanding. Initially, the priorities of Polish diplomacy were to attain recognition for its western border and combat the still-active anti-communist opposition. Regions outside Europe, including Latin America, were not treated as important areas of engagement. In those regions, Poland's focus was mainly on trade, and scientific and cultural cooperation, since these were the most politically neutral fields, although "in the PPR era, in relations with Latin America ideological criteria did affect Polish diplomatic activities, though much less so than in the case of other Soviet bloc countries" (Spyra 2006: 386). Contacts with left-wing governments were preferred and, when forming relations with Latin America, Poland consulted Moscow. Poland did, though, avoid providing direct support for revolutionary movements or becoming involved in socialist internationalism.

Ideological criteria ceased to be considered after 1989. Poland concentrated on strengthening processes of democratisation, building the free market, and guaranteeing its own security in the new geopolitical order. Its main goals were to obtain membership in the European Union (EU) and North Atlantic Treaty Organization (NATO), and so, once again, policy on Latin America was placed on the back burner. There was no coherent conception of Poland's policy in this regard, and so only ad hoc or short-term activities were implemented. At the same time, the states of Latin America emerging from the "lost decade" and, like Poland, setting out on the path towards democracy, were not much interested in maintaining relations with Central and Eastern Europe, which they perceived mainly in the context of rivalry over investment and developmental aid (Spyra 2006: 387). At the beginning of the 1990s, both Poland and the countries of Latin America focused on a series of internal transformations, both political and eco-nomic, and engaged in processes of regional integration. At the same time, a rel-ative weakening of the position of the USA in the western hemisphere translated into greater independence in the policies of Latin American countries, which sought to create international alliances, especially among the emerging powers, and to diversify their economic partnerships.

From the Polish perspective, EU membership obligated it to become more active outside Europe, while the consequences of the financial crisis of 2008 spurred it to seek new economic partners and markets beyond the traditional areas of interest of Polish foreign policy.

Relations with developing countries, though, never became a priority objec-tive. After 1945, Poland's relations with non-European countries were deter-mined by the country's alliance with the USSR and the resulting fact that policy was based on Marxist-Leninist ideology. For its relations with developing states were strictly dependent on its relations with the USSR, and on the evolution of the situation in the latter's non-European dependent territories. Justyna Zając and Ryszard Zięba distinguish three main stages in Poland's relations with the Third World: (1) 1945–1955, covering Poland's activities during the first stage of decolonisation and the resolution of conflicts in areas that process concerned; (2) 1955–1981, a period characterised by support for decolonisation and the development of cooperation with newly independent states; (3) 1981–1989, when cooperation with those states became limited, after which an attempt was made to rebuild them (Zając, Zięba 2005: 194).

In the first years after the end of the World War II, Polish diplomacy focused mainly on supporting the aspirations of colonial nations for independence and seeking resolutions of the conflicts ongoing in those areas. Continuing this direction of engagement, from the mid-1950s official political, economic, and cultural contacts were established with the newly arising post-colonial states, while beginning in 1956, after what is known as the October crisis, solidarity with those countries fighting for independence became one of the three main principles of Polish foreign policy, along with its alliance with the USSR and cooperation with other socialist states, and peaceful coexistence with the countries of the West (Zając, Zięba 2005: 35).

Under the governments of Edward Gierek, those principles were raised to the constitutional level, and laid out in an amendment to the constitution in 1976. Art. 6 of this fundamental legislation stated: "In its policy, the Polish People's Republic: 1) is guided by the interests of the Polish Nation, its sovereignty, independence and security, the will for peace and cooperation among nations; 2) invokes the lofty tradition of solidarity with the powers of freedom and progress, reinforces friendship and cooperation with the Union of Soviet Socialist Republics and other socialist states; 3) bases its relations with states having different political systems on the principles of peaceful coexistence and cooperation" (Zając, Zięba 2005: 36). The principle of solidarity with the nations of Asia, Africa, and Latin America in a way replaced the peaceful coexistence with Western states, and after the imposition of martial law in Poland in 1981, faced with deteriorating relations with capitalist countries, Poland began to rebuild the cooperation it had limited in the second half of the 1970s with neutral developing countries.

Beginning in 1985, the international conditions of Poland's foreign policy began to change. The biggest impact came from the reforms in the USSR, specifically Mikhail Gorbachev's policies of glasnost and perestroika. Gradually, an East-West dialogue was rebuilt, and Poland, emerging from isolation, strove to reconnect internationally through a broad range of activities.

Towards the end of the 1980s, the geopolitical situation in Poland changed fundamentally as a result of deep transformations taking place internationally. The erosion of the communist system led to the "Round Table" talks and the success of the opposition in the first, partially free elections in 1989. These created conditions conducive to the creation of a sovereign, independent foreign policy. At the beginning of the 1990s, political transformation was the top priority of the Polish government; this was accompanied by political and economic reforms, including the transition from a centrally planned to a market economy. Poland's top foreign policy goal became to ensure that, in those difficult times of profound change, the country remained secure – both within its immediate neighbourhood and in the global context. Most important, therefore, were: Poland's relationships with Western states, seen as guarantors of security, especially in the case of the USA and NATO; opportunities for political and economic growth; and the reinforcement of Poland's position internationally, to be achieved through membership in the European Communities, and later the European Union. Emphasis was also put on building alliances within the near vicinity, as seen, for example, in the creation of the Weimar Triangle with France and Germany, and in a certain order being achieved in Poland's relations with Russia and other neighbours to the east. The hierarchy of priorities for Poland's international engagement approved at that time was not conducive to a deepening of its relations with Latin America and the Caribbean. One can even state that the period of internal transformation in Poland, and the reorganisation of its foreign policy goals, led to a marginalisation of the Latin American direction and a reduction in the intensity of Poland's engagement in the region after 1989. As a result, no long-term strategy concerning Latin America and the Caribbean was developed, and activities were undertaken in a rather ad hoc or happenstance manner, contributing little to a permanent tightening of relations with the countries in the region. Many of the goals announced during this period remained mere declarations.

The implementation of Poland's main goals of joining NATO in 1999 and the European Union in 2004 implied a series of changes in Polish policy, both internally and internationally. Membership afforded Polish decision-makers with the possibility of developing effective relations with non-European states using EU mechanisms and instruments. At the same time, Poland became in a way obliged to increase its involvement in areas previously neglected in its foreign policy, including Latin America, treated by the European Union as a serious external partner. For the first time since 1989, the Polish Ministry of Foreign Affairs had to develop a strategy towards non-European states, which it published in 2004 under the title "Strategy of the Republic of Poland in relation to non-European developing countries". The document set out, though in quite a general way, the foundations of Poland's policy towards non-European regions of the world, and indicated opportunities for deepening existing political and economic relations.

In addition to the impulse to activate its non-European policy that no doubt stemmed from Poland's membership in the EU, there were other objective factors that favoured paying more attention to such regions. One of these was the need to look for new economic partners and markets for Polish goods. An intensification in the process of globalisation had led to a shift in weight in international cooperation, from purely political issues to problems concerning the economy and trade. At the same time, non-European states were intensively developing their economies and becoming increasingly attractive partners in international relations through alliances such as BRICS (acronym coined for Brazil, Russia, India, China and South Africa)IBSA (dialogue forum of India, Brazil, and South Africa)and MIKTA (Mexico, Indonesia, Republic of Korea, Turkey, and Australia). Poland in turn, as a member of the EU and NATO, also grew in terms of attractiveness and credibility, and this was conducive to deepening its political and economic relations with other countries. By taking part in EU policies, real conditions opened up for strengthening and stabilising Poland's position, not only within the EU itself, but also on the markets of developing countries (Kacperczyk 2005: 205).

Latin American in Polish foreign policy after 1989

After 1989, Poland's foreign policy was comprehensively redefined in the new regional and global situation. The collapse of the socialist bloc in a way forced Poland to adopt new priorities: to guarantee its own security in the new world order, and to look for new political allies by striving to join NATO and the EU. In this context, Latin America receded into the background of the country's foreign policy. The progress being made in Poland's "economisation" meant that its main efforts in Latin America were aimed at ensuring appropriate conditions for deepening economic cooperation. Poland's foreign policy towards the region focused on five main goals: normalising legal and treaty relations; removing visa obligations reciprocally; restoring the interbellum tradition of creating a network of honorary consulates; promoting Poland and trade exchange; and establishing regular contacts at the undersecretary of state level (Rudowski 2014: 91).

After the fall of the Iron Curtain and the end of the bipolar world order, the importance of ideological criteria in Poland's policy towards Latin America diminished. The existing principle of solidarity with nations fighting for national and social liberation from the yoke of colonialism or neocolonialism was largely replaced with the principle of respecting human rights and political freedoms in international relations (Zięba 2010: 17).

There were few factors conducive to Poland conducting an active foreign policy towards Latin America in the 1990s. On the one hand, the end of the bipolar world order created conditions for creating an objective policy not marked by ideology, but, on the other hand, Poland's foreign policy priorities established in the previous era (including, in particular, a Euro-Atlantic and eastern orientation and Poland's relations with its neighbours), and its engagement in internal changes, did not favour the implementation of an effective Latin American policy.

While the main goals of state security policy and the European orientation were universally accepted and clear, there was a lack of priorities or concrete guidelines concerning Poland's activities outside Europe, including in Latin America. Interest in these was confined to a small group of specialists, and did not become the subject of a wider public debate. The lack of an overall policy towards areas of the world beyond Europe meant that Polish diplomacy focused primarily on implementing ad hoc, short-term goals (Spyra 2006: 387). At the same time, little interest was shown by the states of Latin America in Central and Eastern Europe, which they perceived mainly in the context of the rivalry over developmental aid and new investments. After 1989, the main goals of Polish engagement outside Europe were: maintaining good political relations and a regular political dialogue at a high level and cooperating at the foreign minister level; developing economic and trade cooperation, including promoting Polish exports and protecting Polish economic interests; strengthening contacts with Polonia; and supporting the development of scientific and cultural cooperation (Lizak, Spyra 2002: 316).

In the 1990s, the main task of Polish foreign policy with regard to Latin America was the normalisation of mutual relations as broadly understood. In his exposé of 12 September 1989, Prime Minister Tadeusz Mazowiecki said that it was in Poland's interest to cooperate with the newly industrialised states of Latin America (Leszczyński, Kosecki 2001: 12–14). Political relations with the state of the region were orderly, but not dynamic. Although visits at various levels were held, they did not result in the creation of a long-term concept for Polish foreign policy towards Latin America, or to any growth in Poland's activities in the region. This situation was evident in information released annually by the minister of foreign affairs, in which Latin America was treated perfunctorily, or omitted entirely (Wojna 2006: 51–52).

Poland's accession to the European Union on 1 May 2004 qualitatively redefined its relations with Latin America. EU membership had a tremendous effect on how Poland was perceived internationally, increasing its prestige and its potential for exerting political influence. It also strengthened Poland's position among Latin American states, for whom it became a much more valuable partner. It is fair to say that membership in the EU not only created an opportunity for Poland to strengthen its relations with Latin America and take advantage of EU policy mechanisms, but in fact forced Poland to take a more active role in Latin America, both bilaterally and as part of multilateral cooperation.

Relations between the EU and Latin America have a long tradition of cooperation on many levels and a high level of institutionalisation. Poland's accession to the EU resulted in a number of implications for Poland's policy towards the region. Most of all, it meant that Poland came to be seen as an attractive political and economic partner, one that was credible and stable. The instruments and rules of EU trade policy improved access to the Polish market for goods originating in developing countries. Furthermore, a formal and legal change occurred, for by joining the EU Poland withdrew from a number of bilateral agreements and entered into EU understandings. The Polish government became obligated to develop a written strategy with regard to non-European developing countries – the first document in the country's history that was to comprehensively define Poland's foreign policy goals in relation to those countries.

As a result, in 2004, one of the first documents setting out a framework for Poland's involvement in the region was published by the Ministry of Economy and the Ministry of Foreign Affairs, "Strategy of the Republic of Poland with Regard to Non-European Developing Countries". To a large extent, the publication reflected the "economisation" of Polish foreign policy, since it proposed a focus on developing trade relations with selected countries outside Europe, where the real opportunities for cooperation were to be determined by a given country's economic potential, level, and rate of growth, and the level of competitiveness of Poland goods on the foreign market. The document distinguished three groups of goals for Polish foreign policy in this area:

- short-term (to be implemented starting at once): mobilising state institutions due to the need to active non-European policy; promoting economic cooperation among Polish entrepreneurs; and effectively formulating Poland's position, in accordance with its interests, in ongoing matters of EU policy concerning developing countries;
- mid-term (to be implemented within 5–15 years): foreseeing a deepening of economic cooperation with developing countries; increasing trade turnover, investments and the value of services and number of Polish specialists working in this area; reducing Poland's deficit in relations with certain countries; and fully engaging in EU programmes within this scope;
- long-term: aimed at securing Poland's vital interests, including by: ensuring the best possible external conditions for the development of the country's economy and guaranteeing international security, where initiatives concerning non-European areas would serve to strengthen cooperation with NATO and the EU as well as Poland's position in the international community; and increasing Poland's involvement in solving global problems (Strategia… 2004: 11–12).

In that document, Latin America was treated quite perfunctorily. The states of the region were divided into two groups according to their significance to Polish foreign policy. Among the "priority" states were Argentina, Brazil and Chile (the ABC states) and Mexico, while the "important" states included Venezuela and Colombia. This classification was intended to facilitate identifying Polish interests and make it possible to exert real influence on the development of common EU policy mechanisms concerning developing countries. In relation to the priority states, such as Mexico, Poland's efforts were to focus on an "intensive reinforcement of political and economic ties, promotional and informational activities, the formation of cooperation on the principle of partner relationships, the use of numerous multifaceted mechanisms, and increased activity in favour of exports of Polish investments", as well as on the effective use of diplomatic outlets. In turn, cooperation with "important" states was to concentrate on the formation of political and economic ties and the use of mechanisms of cooperation such as training; informational, promotional and educational activities; cooperation among chambers of commerce; and exchanges among economic missions (Strategia… 2004: 6).

Yet, the results achieved under the strategy were not impressive. Formally, the Strategy of the Republic of Poland in relation to non-European developing countries of November 2004 is one of the main documents concerning Poland's global policy. It points above all to the need to strengthen economic cooperation with "priority states" and "important states" outside Europe. Its authors rightly noted that the attainment of Poland's strategic goals, namely NATO accession in 1999 and EU accession in 2004, were conducive to taking on new challenges and rebuilding relations with developing countries that had been neglected in the period of transformation after 1989. The Strategy was approved by the Council of Ministers, and theoretically created a strong mandate and set the direction for various public institutions. Yet the document described the goals, tasks and instruments of the new policy in only a very general way, without indicating sources of additional means of implementing the strategy. It focused on the characteristics of selected states and the determinants of bilateral relations, with the result that its operational value was severely limited. It provided no explanation of how and within what time frame Poland was to improve its relations with selected countries. Further, as a result of the quick changes in government that took place in 2005 and 2007, the document was not implemented – instead, in the years that followed, individual departments of the Ministry of Foreign Affairs worked out separate strategies regarding Asia, Africa and the Middle East. In practice, then, Poland's policy towards developing countries was deprived of a cohesive, comprehensive plan describing Poland's mid-term vision, priorities, goals, resources and instruments (Kugiel 2015: 1).

Poland set out its first long-term foreign policy strategy in 2012, but little space in it was devoted to Latin America. That region ranked behind the dynamically growing markets and regions of Southeast Asia, Africa and the Middle East, as reflected in documents such as "Priorities of Polish Foreign Policy 2012–2016", wherein Europe was deemed most important, and beyond it the Middle East, Asia and North Africa. Latin America was mentioned as the last non-European area of Polish engagement, where the main foreign policy goal was to implement projects pertaining to climate and energy policy, and the most important partners were Argentina, Brazil, Chile, Mexico and Peru, with emphasis on the need to intensify economic ties with those countries.

The current goals of Poland's foreign policy towards Latin America are to maintain a high-level political dialogue; to take an active part in forming EU policy towards Latin America and the Caribbean favouring a deepening of the political partnership; to develop trade and economic cooperation; and to promote Poland in both bilateral and multilateral relations. An important place in Poland's policy towards the state of the region is held by the issues of security and the respect for human rights and democracy. The level of Poland's relations with Latin American countries has a direct impact on its position in the EU (Stosunki Polska-Ameryka Łacińska i Karaiby 2009: 9–10).

Poland is engaged in a lively political dialogue with Latin American states at the highest level. In its relations with most of those countries, there is a mechanism in place for political and economic consultations at the level of undersecretary of state in the Ministry of Foreign Affairs, and the frequency and scope of those meetings are gradually being increased. Cooperation among parliaments is also significant, including bilateral relations at the level of the leaders of both parliamentary chambers, the foreign affairs commission, and parliamentary groups.

The practical implementation of Poland's foreign policy towards the Latin America and the Caribbean region falls within the remit of the Ministry of Foreign Affairs, specifically its America Department, which coordinates cooperation between the Republic of Poland and Latin American and Caribbean states and their organisations, and analyses the internal situations and foreign policies of those states. It also sets priorities and activities aimed at developing bilateral relations with those states in the political, economic and cultural spheres, and participates in developing EU policy towards the region. Another task of the America Department is to supervise those diplomatic representatives accredited in the states of the region, including embassies.

The Foreign Policy Strategy approved by the Council of Ministers is the fundamental document setting out the foreign policy goals for the Republic of Poland

and how they are to be implemented in the years 2017–2021. It also serves to coordinate the activities of governmental administration bodies in relation to Polish foreign policy, and provides a basis on which the Ministry of Foreign Affairs can develop Polish Foreign Policy Assumptions in the coming years and plans for foreign cooperation prepared in other ministries and authorities. It is approved by the Council of Ministers upon a motion by the minister of foreign affairs. The assumptions constitute guidelines for other ministries developing their own plans for cooperation abroad. The document is classified as "restricted". The unit responsible for preparing the Polish Foreign Policy Assumptions is the Department of Foreign Policy Strategy.

In implementing policy towards Latin American states, many other bodies at the state level are also involved, such as the ministries of National Education, Energy, Finance, Science and Higher Education, and Sport and Tourism, as well as local bodies and, increasingly, the private sector. Despite this, Poland's relations with the region of Latin America and the Caribbean remain scant; their hidden potential is not being developed as it might. This is partly because of a limited availability of funds, but also because there is a "tradition" that the Latin American region plays only a small role in Poland's foreign policy.

Officially, "Polish Foreign Policy Priorities 2012–2016" treated Latin America as an important area for state engagement, where "of primary importance are projects within the scope of climate and energy policy, as well as expanding economic relations, especially with Brazil, Argentina, Mexico, Chile and Peru" (Priorytety… 2012: 20), but it is hard to find confirmation of Latin America's high importance in the yearly publications of the Ministry of Foreign Affairs on Polish foreign policy assumptions, where the region is mentioned only perfunctorily. In the years following the publication of the above document, Latin America remained a region to which Polish foreign policy paid little interest.

Only in 2015, in an exposé by Foreign Minister Grzegorz Schetyna, were a number of references made to cooperation between Poland and the states of Latin America and the Caribbean. Schetyna emphasised that Poland's role in forming the external policy of the EU also obliged it to become more active outside Europe, that if it remained passive and limited its efforts only to its own region, it would become marginalised in international relations. In turn, recognising the economic potential of non-European countries and their growing importance in the world, a need was seen to undertake coordinated, systematic activities in four key areas: 1) political dialogue, aimed at building lasting, multi-dimensional bilateral relations with non-European partners; 2) increased activity within the EU's policy towards those regions; 3) relations with non-European regional organisations, with which substantive, long-term cooperation should be established; 4) consensus-building among Polish political, local governmental, academic and economic circles on the global priorities of Polish foreign policy (Informacja… 2015).

In the years 2016–2017, however, references to Latin America in foreign policy documents again became fewer. The region was mentioned in Poland's foreign policy foundations mainly with regard to the economy and the need to diversify economic partners: "from this imperative arises the idea of a strategic partnership with non-European nations… The current government will therefore consistently support the development of economic cooperation with partners outside Europe. We will increase cooperation, including economic cooperation, with the countries of Latin America and the Caribbean. This should support democratic transformation, economic and social stability, progress in liberalising trade with the EU, and the strong, solidly established presence of Polonia in the region." (Minister Witold Waszczykowski on Polish diplomatic priorities 2016). One year later, there also appeared a declaration of will in the document to give Poland's partnership with Mexico a strategic dimension, and to increase cooperation with the member states of the Pacific Alliance (PA) (Minister Witold Waszczykowski on Polish diplomatic priorities in 2017).

In 2018, when presenting the main foundations of Polish foreign policy for the current year, Foreign Minister Jacek Czaputowicz referred to Latin America only peripherally, stating that "we will develop political and economic cooperation with the states of Latin America and the Caribbean. A basis for optimism is provided by the stable economic and social situation in the leading countries of the region and the progress made in liberalising trade with the European Union". Apart from information on the opening of an embassy in Panama, this was the only mention made of Latin America (Minister Jacek Czaputowicz on Polish diplomatic priorities in 2018).

The document that sets out a framework for Poland's foreign policy activities in the coming years is "Polish Foreign Policy Strategy 2017–2021", in which it is stated that the main tasks will be centred on three interrelated priorities: a) security, that is, activities serving to expand Poland's own defensive capabilities and strengthen the potential of Poland's allies within NATO and the EU; b) an active regional policy; and c) development – international activities serving economic and social development and international authority, understood as a factor making it possible to create a positive image of Poland and strengthen its credibility within Europe and globally. The document also states that "without resigning from having a strong position in the European Union and Eastern Europe, Poland should strengthen economic relations with countries in other regions of the world – South Asia, North and South America, Africa, the Middle East and Australia – as well as with selected developing countries" (Polish Foreign Policy Strategy…: 5). The strategy also announces a change in the geography of Poland's economic activity in the world that should be reflected in an adjustment to the network of Polish diplomatic and consular outlets, and in the direction of trade missions.

Assuming that the degree of liberalisation of world trade has brought beneficial results to the Polish economy, the document states that Poland will support the negotiation of EU free trade agreements with various countries around the world, and that, where it is in line with its interests, Poland will act within this scope in international organisations, particularly the World Trade Organisation (WTO), the Organisation for Economic Co-operation and Development (OECD), the World Bank and the United Nations (UN) agendas.

Among the main tasks to be implemented are:

– activities favouring an increase in the share of highly processed goods among Polish exports;
– efforts to increase the volume of Polish exports of raw materials, particularly black coal;
– activities favouring the creation of international understandings with countries of South Asia, North and South America, the Middle East and Australia, based on common goals within the scope of the use of raw materials, particularly black coal;
– support for the geographical diversification of Polish economic activity globally, with emphasis on the development of cooperation with the countries of Asia, Africa, the Middle East and Latin America;
– the pursuit of provisions beneficial to Poland in trade agreements negotiated by the EU;
– the search for opportunities for cooperation with non-European partners;
– the continuation of activities favouring the identification and elimination of barriers particularly cumbersome for Polish exports seeking access to non-EU markets;
– support for international activities, particularly those undertaken in the forum of the World Trade Organisation, that serve to strengthen the global system of trade in accordance with Poland's economic interest;
– activities favouring an increase in foreign visitors by promoting innovative tourism products (Strategia 2017: 18–20).

Latin America again receives little attention, being treated as an element of the broader group of non-European countries towards which Polish foreign policy should concentrate on diversifying political contacts and strengthening economic cooperation.

There are no contentious issues between Poland and the states of Latin America, and historically, political relations between them have been good, which facilitates a deeper dialogue with a number of countries in the region (in addition to Mexico, these include Argentina, Chile, Peru and Colombia) through political and economic consultations at the vice-ministerial level. In the years 2016–2017, the efforts of Polish diplomacy were focused on stepping up political relations with the above countries, as confirmed by, for example, by Poland's offer to cooperate in connection with its status as an observer in the PA and its establishment of a stronger dialogue with Mexico.

According to the Ministry of Foreign Affairs, among the factors that determine the importance of Latin America and the Caribbean for Poland, those most often mentioned are: shared Christian and democratic values; allegiance to the rules of international law and the need to enforce them; a shared cultural and historical legacy; and the large Polish diaspora, members of which have a presence in governing elites in the region. The Ministry also emphasises that a tightening of relations with Latin America and the Caribbean will serve to diversify markets and globalise Polish foreign policy; this reinforces Poland's position within the European Union, whose presence in Latin America constitutes a counterbalance to Chinese and American expansion. The Latin America and the Caribbean region is also an important element on the international scene, and an active participant in global competition; Latin American states such as Mexico belong to the exclusive G-20 group and are member states of the OECD.

Further, in the context of diversifying Polish exports, the market of Latin America and the Caribbean, with more than 600 million inhabitants and a growing middle class, is extremely attractive, while the relative stability of the region provides plenty of opportunities for economic cooperation with Polish entrepreneurs. Another positive factor is the fact that the EU possesses a free trade zone with almost half the continent (SICA, Mexico, Chile, a multilateral trade agreement with Peru and Colombia), while there is a great need in the countries of the region to develop cooperation on agricultural and food, road and rail infrastructure, social housing, renewable energy sources and water management. Global players are also attracted by Latin America's abundant natural resources. On the political level, Latin America and the Caribbean are an important partner in the dialogue on climate change and environmental protection, the principles of sustainable development and the protection of human rights. Within the UN system, Poland exchanges support with Latin American countries for positions and candidates in international organisations.

Recently, Poland has intensified cooperation on developing treaties, beginning from agreements in the nature of political memoranda to specific understandings on, for example, the transfer of convicts, extradition, Work and Holiday, cooperation on tourism and sport, cooperation on the protection of cultural, scientific and technological goods, the exchange of financial information, and cooperation in Antarctica.

The growing importance of the region in Poland's foreign policy is attested to by a document issued by the Ministry of Foreign Affairs Department of America in 2015, titled "Foreign Policy Challenges of the Republic of Poland regarding Latin America and the Caribbean (2015–2020 and after 2020)". The document is not an interpretation of the position of the Foreign Ministry, but rather an attempt to address the main foundations of Poland's policy towards Latin American countries and the most important instruments for shaping that policy. It also outlines possibilities for political and economic cooperation with the states of the region, emphasising both the opportunities for and threats to the development of mutual relations. In it, two groups of states are distinguished – "key" states and "returning partners". The main goals of Polish foreign policy towards the region continue to be to diversify markets and guarantee economic security, as well as to enhance Poland's position within the EU and in the international arena. In turn, the political goals include continuing the political dialogue and striving to obtain support in international institutions for Polish positions and candidates. Along with Argentina and Brazil, Mexico found itself among the key partners, due to its trade potential and global engagement. In bilateral relations, a recommendation has been made to make trade contacts and the political dialogue top priorities, while at the same time developing cooperation in the areas of culture, education, and science and technology. The document identifies tasks for Poland's foreign policy towards Latin America and the Caribbean in the short term (2015–2016), mid term (2017–2020) and long term (after 2020), as well as the main tools for implementing these.

Short-term tasks include increasing Poland's diplomatic presence in Latin America and the Caribbean, strengthening political relations with Central America and members of the PA and Brazil, and revitalising the political dialogue with Cuba. These goals may be achieved by: reactivating diplomatic representation in Central America (which took place in 2017, when a Polish embassy was opened in Panama); obtaining observer status in the PA (achieved in 2015) and CARICOM (the Caribbean Community and Common Market); increasing cooperation on development within the small grant system; expanding the base of legal treaties with Latin American states; deepening cultural, scientific and research cooperation; and enhancing Poland's image. On the economic level, the main short-term goals include attracting direct investments from Latin America; supporting the expansion of Polish businesses on the Latin American market; and revitalising economic cooperation through economic missions in the states of the region, promotional campaigns and EU mechanisms for economic cooperation and information sharing.

The most important mid- and long-term goals include increasing Poland's economic security, and strengthening its position as an important political partner for Latin American states and as an important entity shaping EU policy in the region. The main instruments for achieving this are: improving coordination between the Ministry of Foreign Affairs and other ministries; ensuring an appropriate frequency of meetings at the highest level; and making sure Poland plays an active part in developing and implementing EU policy towards Latin America.

Poland is active in developing and implementing EU policy towards the region (at the COLAC forum and in other EU bodies), including in the context of preparing for negotiations on modernising the EU-Mexico and EU-Chile agreements, ratifying the EU-Cuba agreement on dialogue and cooperation, negotiating the trade part of the EU association agreement with Mercosur, and ratifying the agreement on establishing an EU-LAC Foundation. Every two years, Poland takes part in summits at the level of heads of states and governments organised by the EU and the Community of Latin American and Caribbean States.

After 2012, Poland's Latin American policy focused mainly on building up economic relations, especially with those states deemed as priority states, including Mexico; acting to bring the EU's agreements with Central America, Peru and Colombia into force; and continuing the EU-Mercosur association agreement. In 2015–2016, in turn, Poland's foreign policy efforts in Latin America were aimed at intensifying political relations with members of the PA; in 2015, this led to Poland obtaining observer status at the organisation, and to its establishing a stronger dialogue with Mexico.

One of the weaknesses of Poland's foreign policy towards the states of Latin America, however, remains the lack of frequency of political contacts and their low level of institutionalisation. Poland does not make full use of the instruments of EU policy towards non-European states, for example, developmental aid. Even though it emphasises in its official rhetoric that it uses the system of small grants, in practice this became the case only after 2007, when several projects were begun that also extended to Latin American states (Gawrycki 2010: 240). Polish developmental aid, within this scope and seen against other European states, is very small and makes only a small contribution to building up Poland's image among the countries of Latin America.

***

Poland's foreign policy towards Latin America is based on three pillars: political, economic and cultural-social, where a key role is also played by contact with Latin American Polonia circles. Despite the official rhetoric, in which the Latin America and the Caribbean region is given an important place, in reality it occupies a marginal position in Poland's international activities. A certain impetus was given to Poland's engagement in the region when Poland acceded to the EU: on the one hand, this provided access to EU mechanisms for cooperating with Latin America already developed, and on the other hand obligated Poland to define its goals and expectations in respect of the region. Another event that, to a certain extent, made Polish decision-makers aware of the significance of their Latin American partners was the economic crisis that began in 2008. At that time, Latin America began to be perceived as a region of stable, relatively predictable states and of alternative markets, especially in the context of the economic and political crisis in which Europe was entangled.

There are, then, certain positive signals as to the growing importance of the region in Poland's foreign policy. The lack of a tradition of close contacts means that the process of making the declared partnership a reality will be a long one; yet it will definitely be beneficial for all parties concerned.

I Political relations

History of Polish-Mexican relations

Poland and Mexico – two states that at first glance would seem to have more dividing than uniting them – are closer to each other than it seems. Not only their geography, but also their histories have not been conducive to the development of bilateral relations between them. In the policy of Poland, Mexico (unlike the Dominican Republic or Colombia) was not seen as a suitable place for organised Polish colonisation, with the result that Poland paid little attention to it. During the time of the first Polish Republic, Mexico was a colony of Spain, and when Mexico was fighting for independence at the beginning of the 19th century, Poland was partitioned among Russia, Austro-Hungary and Prussia, wiped off the map of sovereign states for more than 100 years. And at the time Poland regained its independence in 1918, Mexico was mired down in chaos and the consequences of the Mexican Revolution, which redefined the country's priorities internationally.

The first contacts between the two states date back to the 16th century. Information on the conquest of the New World came to Poland almost first-hand. A Polish diplomat at the Spanish court, Jan Dandyszek, exchanged letters with Hernán Cortés, who described the land, people and customs of the areas he conquered. Thus, not only the stages of the conquest, but also the specific nature, cultural diversity and geography of the New World were followed.

From 1795 to 1918, when Poland was absent from maps of the world as a result of having been partitioned, Polish-Mexican relations were determined by the policies of the partitioning powers – Prussia, Austria and Russia – towards Mexico. It is worth recalling that Prussia was the most interested of the three in establishing trade relations. The frequency with which Silesia appears in studies relating to Polish-Mexican relations permits the hypothesis that it was in these Polish lands, under Prussian domination, that information on Mexico penetrated most, and from which, over time, direct contacts with Mexico were established in the first half of the 19th century (Smolana 2018: 225).

As Tadeusz Łepkowski writes, "certain similarities of fate meant that some members of the elites of these two lands, so distant from each other, developed a mutual interest and sympathy in the late 18th and early 19th centuries" (Łepkowski 1970: 76). From 1827 to 1832, the Head of the Trade Agency in Paris, who was in practice as a diplomatic representative of the Mexican Republic, was Tomás Murphy. In the reports he sent to the Ministry of Foreign Affairs, he often mentioned his sympathy for the Poles in their struggle for independence, emphasising their devotion and the unequal fight they were waging against the partitioning powers (Łepkowski 1970: 76–77). Mexicans from Tampico even took up a collection, raising 5,000 francs for Polish emigrants in France (Lerski 1958: 53). In the years 1870–1918, however, Polish-Mexican contacts weakened significantly (Łepkowski 1970: 86), mainly because of the difficulties Poles in Mexico had in maintaining contact with their compatriots at home under the rule of the three occupying powers.

A new stage in Polish-Mexican relations began only when Poland regained its independence in 1918. As a result of the political reality of the time, bilateral relations were properly established, but were not among the best. Many differences existed between the principles that guided the pro-revolutionary Mexican authorities and those of the Polish authorities, especially after the May Coup.

Mexico officially recognised Poland on 1 September 1921. On 5 June 1922, the first officials of the Mexican Ministry of Foreign Affairs came to Poland – Rodolfo Nervo and Julio Pani – on a mission to thank the Polish government for sending a delegation to the celebrations for the 100th anniversary of Mexican independence. This high-level visit was in line with the political reality of the time, where post-revolutionary Mexico was isolated in the international arena, and the goal of Poland's foreign policy was to establish a network of diplomatic contacts as dense as possible with the states of Latin America. Historians regard the invitation to the centennial anniversary of independence as Mexico's unofficial recognition of Polish independence. In turn, the presence of representatives of Poland at the celebrations is understood as Poland's recognition of Mexico's independence (Moleznick 2007: 120).

The most important reason why formal and legal bilateral relations were not finally established was the internal situation in Mexico. There were fears in Poland over the revolutionary character of the country, associated with lawlessness, political chaos, anti-clericalism and xenophobia, evident, for example, in the conflict between the Mexican government and the Catholic Church, known as the "guerrra de los Cristeros" (1926–1929). Poland's relations with Mexico were also affected by the reluctance shown by the United States and the Vatican becoming closer to them.

In the early years of Poland's independence, the development of official diplomatic relations was hindered by geographical distance, the language barrier and, probably most importantly, the limited financial resources of the two countries. They could not afford to set up appropriate representation. That impasse lasted until 1928, when it was finally decided to establish official diplomatic relations at the envoy level. On 14 June 1928, a Polish Consulate General was opened in Mexico City, headed by Zygmunt Merdinger. And on 8 February 1929, a Mexican Consulate General was opened in Warsaw, headed by Raúl Rodriguez Duarte. Thus, Mexico became the third Latin American country – after Brazil and Argentina – to establish diplomatic relations with Poland.

These events, however, did not amount in practice to an intensification of bilateral relations. Interstate contacts were limited to exchanges of correspondence and depeches sent out of courtesy. That the two states did not consider bilateral relations between them as a priority is evident from the fact that in the interbellum period, they did not sign any significant agreements, even though in the same period Mexico was intensively building trade relations with, for example, Czechoslovakia and other Central and Eastern European states. Tadeusz Łepkowski distinguished three main stages in the political relations between Poland and Mexico between the two world wars: sporadic contacts (1921–1927), the formation of lasting diplomatic relations (1928–1931) and a short period of institutionalised relations at a rather low level (1932–1939) (Łepkowski 1980: 77).

One factor that in a way forced the two countries to maintain friendly relations was the growing number of people migrating from Poland to Mexico. As mentioned earlier, Polish envoys in Mexico City began to function only in 1929. Polish emigrants, of whom quite a number moved to Mexico during the interbellum period, were thus deprived of diplomatic care for a long time. It is estimated that in this period, about 600 Poles a year moved to Mexico, many of whom were of Jewish origin, or Silesians belonging to the Salesians of Don Bosco order (Łepkowski 1970: 88). In 1930, it was estimated that 2,142 Poles had emigrated to Mexico, of whom about 2,000 were Jews. They settled mainly in urban centres and quickly became naturalised – in 1935 fewer than 1,200 of them still held Polish citizenship (Łepkowski 1970: 88).

A new element in Polish-Mexican contacts during the interbellum period was a gradual development of trade relations. No formal agreement on trade exchange was signed, and the amount of trade was not large, but it gradually paved the way towards the development of those relations later on. There was visible growth in trade exchange in the years 1932–1935, in part because of the engagement of Polonia in Mexico. In 1934, a special company was established for trading with Poland – Compañía Mercantil Transmarítima – and in 1935 the Gulf Gdynia Line began sailing from Poland to Tampico. The largest turnover was seen in 1934, when Polish exports to Mexico were worth 1.5 million zlotys, and imports almost 1.1 million (Łepkowski 1970: 89). Exports consisted mainly of plywood, paraffin, cigarette paper, gloves, kitchen utensils and brewer's barley. Imports from Mexico included coffee, sisal agave fibres, zincblende, etc. (Łepkowski 1970: 89).

An important role in increasing the closeness of Polish-Mexican relations in the interbellum period was played by Zbigniew Merdinger, the Republic of Poland's diplomatic representative in Mexico. He strove to create a Polish lobby in Mexico, centred on the Friends of Poland Society (Sociedad Amigos de Polonia) established in 1933 and headed by the geologist Esequiel Ordoñez, president of the Sociedad Mexican de Geografía y Estadística and an advisor to the Mexican Oil Association (Smolana 2018: 271). Within the scope of promoting bilateral trade, he also published a book encouraging the development of economic contacts and outlining the characteristics of the two markets and the benefits they offered to potential investors.

Proper political relations were established, though a number of potentially thorny issues did exist. As Tadeusz Łepkowski writes: "If they were not good, it was mainly because of the Polish authorities' cool reserve towards Mexico. Mexican's progressive government was criticised openly in Poland; during the 1920 for anti-clericalism, and during the Cardenas era for socialism" (Łepkowski 1970: 90). That perception gradually evolved: "in an overall assessment of Mexico's attitude towards Poland and Poland's towards Mexico, one must distinguish between the twenties and the thirties. Generally, one can say that, initially, the Mexican government – despite aggressive, anti-Polish German propaganda – looked on Poland quite favourably, though it knew little about the country. The Republic, on the other hand... distanced itself from Mexico because of Mexico's revolutionary tendencies, and especially its anti-clericalism. In the 1930s, Mexico wanted to maintain good relations with all states, but had misgivings about Poland as a state led by a pro-totalitarian, or even a pro-fascist, government. For its part, Poland took a dim view of Mexican leftist extremism and the government's pro-Soviet tendencies" (Łepkowski 1980: 92).

During this period, there were a mere two exceptions from the general rule of friendship and goodwill. The first was a three-year period (1927–1929) marked by a conflict between the Mexican state and the Church, known as the Cristero Rebellion. The rebellion was directed against the government, which was implementing the anti-clerical provisions of the Mexican Constitution of 1917. Initially, the resistance of the "cristeros" was peaceful, but as the process of secularisation introduced by President Plutarco Elías Calles intensified, in 1927 it took the form of a regular war against the forces of the state. About 90,000 people lost their lives in the Cristeros Rebellion. In Poland, a Catholic country, the measures taken by the Mexican authorities were presented in a very negative light, which discouraged any tightening of bilateral relations.

Another episode that pushed the two states apart was a short-lived misunderstanding between Polish and Mexican delegates to the League of Nations in 1936 on the question of Abyssinia. Mexico and Poland took up completely opposite positions on this issue, and this was especially visible at the League of Nations. Mexico favoured the imposition of sanctions on Italy, and coordinated the "Committee of Eighteen" states. After the annexation of Abyssinia in May 1936, when the League failed to comply with Mexico's objection to the lifting of sanctions, Mexico withdrew from the Committee in protest. At the same time, Mexico objected to the idea of removing Ethiopia's representation from the League of Nations and recalling its political representatives from Rome (Antonia Pi-Suñer, Paolo Riguzzi, Lorena Ruano 2011: 304–305). Whereas Poland, despite initial, timid attempts to support the Ethiopian government, finally took up a pro-Italian position, as attested to in 1937 by the change in the competencies of the Polish Consulate General in Rome to include Ethiopia, which could be read as a tacit acknowledgment of Italy's takeover (Degefe Demechu 2006: 179).

In the area of cultural and academic relations, though there were few contacts, they gradually developed; this was mainly due, though, to the individual and social initiatives, and not to steps taken by government. In the interbellum period, Dr Wacław Górczyński conducted meteorological research in Mexico; he also co-organized the creation of an observatory with Dr Zenon Lemański. During World War II, Prof. Feliks Sobota conducted studies on volcanoes.

In 1938, faced with the inevitability of a German invasion of Poland, the diplomatic representatives of Mexico were moved to Anin, near Warsaw; when the war broke out, they moved again to Kazimierz on the Vistula, and finally, along with the Polish government, to Bucharest. Luciano Joublanc Rivas, Mexico's chargé d'affaires ad interim in Poland, was at that time the only Latin American diplomat who stayed with the Polish government up to the end of the fighting. During the war, diplomatic contacts were maintained through Mexico's envoy to the Norwegian and Polish governments in London, and the military attaché of the Polish government-in-exile in Washington. News of the wartime events in Poland, such as the Warsaw Uprising, reached Mexico and were given wide coverage there in the press.

In December 1942, General Władysław Sikorski went to Mexico on behalf of the Polish government-in-exile; he and President Manuel Ávila Camacho agreed conditions for the acceptance of Polish refugees from camps in the Middle East. The refugees landed on Mexican soil in two contingents, in July and November of the following year, and were placed in the Santa Rosa colony in the state of Guanajuato. In this way, Mexico became the only country in the Americas that provided support for Polish refugees. In 1944, the Provisional Government of National Unity that arose in Poland (supported by the Soviet Union) led to a rupture in relations with the Polish government-in-exile and the closure of the camp in 1946.

On 9 July 1944, Mexico was the first Latin American country to recognise the Provisional Government of National Unity and to appoint special envoys and ministerial plenipotentiaries – Jan Drohojowski in Mexico and Luciano Joublanc Rivas in Warsaw. That change was made only with great difficulty, since the diplomats of the Polish government in London considered themselves the official representatives of Poland and sent aid to the Polish colony in Mexico.

Policy of the Polish People's Republic (PPR) towards Mexico

Marcos Pablo Moloeznik distinguishes three main periods in Polish-Mexican relations during the Cold War era. The first is characterised by friendly bilateral relations: from the mutual recognition of the governments and highest authorities to the crisis in the years 1945/46. Generally speaking, the diplomats of both countries cooperated with each other. An example of this was in April 1946 when, at the request of the Poland's representative at the UN, Oskar Lange, the representative of Mexico, Francisco Castillo Nájera, submitted a motion to break off diplomatic relations with the government of General Francisco Franco in Spain. At the same time, the Polish Foreign Minister Wincenty Rzymowski visited Mexico to take part in the swearing-in ceremony of Miguel Alemán Valdez (1946–1952). This was the first, and in fact the only, high-level mission in Poland's relations with Latin America during the 1940s. (Dumała 1997: 13).

The second period, from 1947 to the 1950s, coincided with the increasing conflict between East and West, and led to a gradual loss of contact between Poland and Mexico. The logic of the Cold War meant that, not only did Polish-Mexican relations not flourish, but in Mexico steps were taken to isolate the Polish colony from its diplomatic representation. The governments of Miguel Alemán Valdes and Adolfo Ruiz Cortinez (1952–1958) were marked by a strong anti-communism, while the regime's establishment of a political police force – the National Security Directorate (1947–1985) – and fears of possible repressions weakened the ties between Poles living in Mexico and their country of origin. This stage of obscurantism largely came to an end with a visit to Poland in 1958 by the former president of Mexico, Lázaro Cárdenas. He was met by the Chairman of the State Council, Aleksander Zawadzki, and this initiated a new, more balanced stage in bilateral relations (Moloeznik 2007: 141).

Only in the 1960s was there a gradual normalisation and intensification of political relations. In its diplomatic practice, Poland began to move away from permanent missions at the envoy level and, by 1960, had raised its representation in Mexico to that of an embassy. Mexico was also the only Latin American country that Polish Prime Minister Józef Cyrankiewicz visited, in 1963. In the same year, Mexican President Adolfo López Mateos (1958–1964) paid a return visit to Warsaw. In this period, Mexico was one of six Latin American countries (along with Brazil, Chile, Colombia, Cuba and Venezuela) with which Poland maintained relations through high-level special missions (Dumała 1997: 14). Those relations included visits to Mexico by: the Polish minister of foreign affairs, Adam Rapacki, in 1964; the minister of shipping, Stanisław Darski, in 1960 – who took part in the celebrations of the 150th anniversary of the proclamation of Mexican independence; the minister of foreign affairs, Emil Wojtaszek, in 1977; and the chairman of the State Council, Henryk Jabłoński, in 1979.

In the decades that followed, purely ceremonial missions also took place. In 1970, the chairman of the State Council, Mieczysław Klimaszewski, took part in the celebrations of the swearing-in of President Luis Echeverría Álvarez; in 1976, there was a special mission by the deputy chairman of the State Council, Zdzisław Tomala, to the celebrations of the takeover of power by President-elect José López Portillo (Dumała 1997: 15).

Generally, however, during the Cold War, political relations between Poland and Mexico were merely of a formal nature involving official visits. It is hard to speak of any real understanding between the states being built, since they were divided by ideology and their affiliation with camps hostile towards each other. One has the impression that political relations were maintained for PR reasons only, for the only real cooperation going on at the time was a gradual expansion of the sphere of economic contacts. Devoid of controversy and not burdened with ideological differences, cultural relations gradually came to be another realm in which the two states could achieve some kind of real rapprochement.

Poland's policy towards Mexico after 1989

Perhaps surprisingly, after the end of the Cold War and the political transformation in Poland, no large changes were seen in Poland's foreign policy towards Mexico, or more broadly, Latin America as a whole. Mexico – as in the past – is now seen as a priority country in the region, both economically and politically. The official rhetoric serves to maintain good relations between the two states, but is not accompanied by any intensive direct contacts. Since 1963, when Józef Cyrankiewicz visited Mexico, high-level visits there have been sporadic. Only in 1998, there was another visit by a Polish Prime Minister, Jerzy Buzek, during which a number of bilateral understandings were signed on such issues as avoiding double taxation, abolishing the visa regime, and scientific and technological cooperation. At the same time, in order to facilitate exchanges of information between officials of their embassies, the two countries started up Meetings of the Mechanism for Consultations on the Common Interest (Reunión de Mecanismo de Consultas de Interés Común) (Moloeznik 2007: 130).

In the first decade of the new century, there was a noticeable increase in the intensity of bilateral relations. This was due in part to Poland being positively perceived in Mexico as a leader in its region with considerable international potential, in line with its European integration (Bogdziewicz 2002: 229–230). In 2002, Mexico was visited by the Polish vice premier and minister of finance, Marek Belka, and the secretary of state of the Ministry of Internal Affairs and Administration, Zbigniew Sobotka. During the visit, an agreement was signed on combating organised crime and other forms of crime, and preliminary talks were held on cooperation within the scope of supplies of military equipment. Further, as part of supplementing the treaty basis between the two states, Poland ratified the convention on avoiding double taxation, and opened an honorary consulate in Acapulco. In 2003, on the occasion of the 75th anniversary of the establishment of diplomatic relations, Mexico was visited by the Polish minister of foreign affairs, Włodzimierz Cimoszewicz, and Poland hosted two Mexican ministers of foreign affairs – Rosario Green in 2000 and José Antonio Meade Kuribreña in 2015. During the last of these visits, progress was made on cooperation to intensify political, economic and cultural relations. At that time, the Polish Foreign Minister, Grzegorz Schetyna, sent a letter of intent requesting that Poland be granted observer status at the PA, a request that was granted in the same year.

The first visit to Poland in many years by a Mexican President – in this case, Vicente Fox – took place in 2004. The formal and legal result of the trip was the Agreement concluded between the Government of the Republic of Poland and the United States of Mexico on Cooperation in the Field of Tourism. It was also decided to create a joint commission charged with identifying factors impeding bilateral cooperation and with specifying activities and directions in which economic contacts could be deepened. During the visit, the Polish President, Aleksander Kwaśniewski, was awarded Mexico's Order of the Aztec Eagle in recognition of his contribution to improving Polish-Mexican relations. From that time, it was another 13 years before the first-ever visit by a Polish president to Mexico, when Andrzej Duda travelled there in 2017.

The bilateral political dialogue is maintained by the Mechanism of Political Consultations (MPC) established pursuant to a memorandum concluded in 1998. Within the MPC, meetings are held for the purpose of evaluating various aspects of Polish-Mexican bilateral relations. The 11th round of consultations took place in June 2018. It was emphasised then that Poland and Mexico share similar values and take similar positions on many issues, such as the need to strengthen democracy and the rule of law, the protection of human rights, energy security and free trade. It was also pointed out that in implementing the agreement concluded during the visit by President Andrzej Duda, particular attention should be paid to economic matters[1]. The frequency of meetings of the commission, however, is not defined, which considerably limits the effectiveness of the mechanism[2].

Within the scope of bilateral cooperation, one institutionalised instrument of dialogue is the Joint Commission for Educational and Cultural Cooperation between Poland and Mexico, established pursuant to an intergovernmental Agreement on Cooperation in the Fields of Education and Culture of 1997. Sessions of the commission should take place once every four years, alternately in Warsaw and Mexico City, and their purpose is to approve executive programmes concerning bilateral cooperation in the fields of education and culture. In recent years, these meetings have been held in the form of teleconferences.

After 1990, a mechanism for political and economic consultations was also introduced at the undersecretary of state and expert think-tank levels. Their activities are to focus on monitoring bilateral relations between the two sides and preparing an annual report (Miodek 2009: 27).

Bilateral cooperation also takes place at the parliamentary level. Since 1992, within the Polish Parliament, a Polish-Mexican Parliamentary Group has functioned (Rynkowska 2007: 152). In 2015, the subject of the first official visit to Mexico in fourteen years by the Polish-Mexican parliamentary group included economic, educational, cultural and local government cooperation. The central point of the visit was a meeting with the Mexico-Poland Friendship Group (Grupo de Amistad México-Polonia) of the Chamber of Deputies of the Mexican Congress. Polish delegates also met with representatives of Polonia and Mexican government institutions. Since then, direct contacts at this level have intensified, as attested to by the fact that, in June 2016, the Foreign Affairs Committees of the Polish and Mexican Senates signed a Memorandum on Cooperation and Dialogue. In April 2017, in turn, the Mexican Senate organised a photographic

---

1 Polish-Mexican political consultations, 14 June 2018, https://msz.gov.pl/pl/aktualnosci/ wiadomosci/polsko_meksykanskie_konsultacje_polityczne;jsessionid=80619E21309B DB4ECD25887E26482BCA.cmsap5p (accessed: 17.06.2018).
2 Previous rounds were held in 1999, 2001, 2003, 2004, 2006, 2007, 2010, 2014, 2015, 2016.

exhibition titled "Polonia, un país de patrimonio mundial", which displayed
Poland's natural and cultural heritage[3]. At the same time, it is worth recalling
that both Poland and Mexico are part of the Inter-Parliamentary Union[4].

Polish-Mexican cooperation also takes place at the local level. Important
tools of Poland's foreign policy towards the region are public and cultural diplomacy, and cooperation at the local government level. Partner cities include
Guadalajara-Wrocław and Kraków, Mérida-Stargard Szczeciński, Puebla-Łódź,
and Tijuana-Słubice. They implement joint projects in many areas.

The two states also have a well-developed network of embassies and consulates.
Up to 2017, the Polish embassy in Mexico also represented Poland's interests in
the countries of Central America. But with the opening of an outlet in Panama,
now only Costa Rica and Mexico are outside of its remit. An agreement of
25 June 2015, the "Consular Law", referred to the tradition of the interbellum
period and also introduced the institution of honorary consul. In exceptional
circumstances, with the consent of the Ministry of Foreign Affairs and the
Ministry of Justice, an honorary consul can perform certain actions notarially, and
provide care to Polish citizens residing abroad. In 2015, 205 honorary consulates
were established, of which the largest number in any country – 13 – were opened
in Mexico (Report by the Polish diplomatic and consular services 2016: 6–7). In
2018, honorary consulates functioned in six Mexican cities: Acapulco, Cancún,
Guadalajara, Guanajuato, Monterrey, Tijuana and Tulancingo[5]. Mexico has five
such consulates in: Kraków, Gdańsk, Poznań, Szczecin and Wrocław.

Apart from their bilateral relations, Poland and Mexico also cooperate at the
multilateral level, including with the EU, UN, OECD and the PA. Their cooperation is particularly fruit in the forum of the United Nations, where they
have very convergent views on many issues. The percentage indicator of that

---

3   Inauguran en el Senado exposición fotográfica "Polonia, un país de patrimonio
    mundial", Boletin, 25.04.2017, http://comunicacion.senado.gob.mx/index.php/
    informacion/boletines/36063-inauguran-en-el-senado-exposicion-fotografica-
    polonia-un-pais-de-patrimonio-mundial.html (accessed: 12.07.2018).
4   The Inter-Parliamentary Union is an organisation gathering together Mps from 178
    parliaments around the world and 12 associate members. It was established in 1889,
    and Poland has been a member since 1921.
5   In 2017, there were loud reverberations among Polonia in Mexico when a Polish hon-
    orary consul, Alberto Stebelski-Orłowski, was recalled after declining to accept the
    Order of Merit of the Republic of Poland from the hands of President Andrzej Duda
    as a sign of protest against developments in the internal situation in Poland. https://
    www.msz.gov.pl/pl/informacje_konsularne/polskie_placowki/placowki.

convergence in the context of Polish and Mexican votes case on resolutions of the 60th UN General Assembly was 64%, with the greatest agreement achieved on such subjects as decolonisation (100%) and the Middle East (88%), and the least on Development (38%) (Recommendations on strengthening relations between Poland and Mexico 2015: 51). Mexico put forward drafts of nine resolutions, of which Poland co-authored three: "United Nations Study on educational programmes for disarmament and containment of nuclear weapons", "Treaty on a total ban on nuclear testing" and "Psychological aggression, intimidation or bullying". Poland also voted in favour of other draft resolutions submitted by Mexico: "Progress in multilateral negotiations on the issue of nuclear disarmament" and "Towards a world free of nuclear arms: accelerating the implementation of obligations undertaken on the issue of nuclear disarmament". For its part, every year Mexico supports drafts put forward by Poland, such as: "Implementation of the convention on a ban on testing, producing, storing and using chemical weapons and on destroying stores thereof". Poland and Mexico also cooperate on implementing the provisions of the Nuclear Weapons Non-Proliferation Treaty in the forum of the Non-Proliferation and Disarmament Initiative (NPDI) (Recommendations: 51). Thanks in part to the support of Mexico, Poland also obtained a mandate as a non-permanent member of the UN Security Council in the years 2018–2019[6]. At the same time, Poland supports the negotiations on a new global agreement between Mexico and the European Union.

Mexico's place in Polish foreign policy

In one of the first documents setting out the scope of Poland's engagement in Latin America, among other areas, that is, the "Strategy of the Republic of Poland in relation to non-European developing countries" approved in 2004, Mexico was treated as a priority country. It was assumed therein that in relation to those countries, Poland should focus on an "intensive reinforcement of political and economic ties, promotional and informational activities, the formation of cooperation on the principle of partner relationships, the use of numerous multifaceted mechanisms, and increased activity in favour of exports of Polish investments", as well as on an effective use of diplomatic outlets (Strategy... 2004: 6). Even though Mexico was mentioned as one of the main addressees

---

6 Previously, Poland exercised a mandate as a non-permanent member of the UN Security Council in the years 1946–47, 1960–61, 1970–71, 1982–83 and 1996–97.

of Poland's strategy, barely two pages of the document were devoted to it. Those factors considered conducive to the development of bilateral coopera- tion included: the revival of the Mexican economy in 2004 after several years of stagnation, its significant deposits of crude oil and natural gas, its relatively stable political and economic system, regular cooperation between Mexico and the EU, and its political and economic dialogue with Poland and relatively well- developed cultural and educational cooperation. Whereas factors perceived as limiting cooperation included Mexico's high level of foreign debt, its deterio- rating internal security, and unsettled contentious issues, such as those con- cerning veterinary regulations. There were also fears of another wave of social unrest in Chiapas. Potential areas for Polish-Mexican cooperation include the energy and electricity sector, the oil and petrochemical industry, and natural gas exploration (Strategy... 2004: 54–55).

Yet, despite its lofty goals, the Strategy did not lead to any real intensification of relations with Mexico. An attempt was made to give those relations a new impetus, and the growing importance of Mexico for Poland was acknowledged, by means of a conference organised under the patronage of the Polish Ministry of Foreign Affairs and the Embassy of Mexico in Poland, titled: "A reinforced Polish-Mexican dialogue: a new opening in bilateral relations", held in September 2016 in Warsaw. At that time, attention was drawn to the need to increase the institutionalisation of mutual relations, as this would make it possible to better define areas of cooperation and work together effectively. It was emphasised that the growing activity of the two states internationally, their desire to improve their global position and ability to act regionally, and their positive economic results all favour the idea of strengthening Polish-Mexican cooperation. During the con- ference, a publication was presented that was the result of consultations between government, the academic community and business, issued under the auspices of the ministries of foreign affairs of the two states: "Recomendaciones para el fortalecimiento de la relación entre México y Polonia. Recommendations on a strengthening of relations between Poland and Mexico". The recommendations it contains were also the subject of the 10th round of political and economic consultations between Poland and Mexico in November 2016. At that time, it was emphasised that the document is the only publication of its kind that Mexico had developed with a European state.

The document defines areas for creating intensive bilateral cooperation, including: heading towards regular, broad exchanges of information and consultations at various levels, which would ensure continuity of joint projects; using the PA and the Visegrad Group as forums for reviving relations with third states; and continuing to cooperate through international organisations on matters where positions are convergent. Also emphasised were the benefits resulting from Poland's membership in the EU, and Mexico's role, due to its geographical location and macroeconomic conditions, as a bridge between Central America and the Caribbean and with many Asia and Pacific region countries (Recommendations 2015: 53).

The purpose of the document is, on the one hand, to outline the current state of relations between Poland and Mexico, and on other hand, to make general and specific recommendations concerning the development of bilateral relations. Those recommendations should guide institutions in both states to take specific measures in the coming years aimed at strengthening the ties between Poland and Mexico in the areas of politics, the economy, and regional and multilateral cooperation.

Potential areas for joint activities include security and combating organised crime; education, music education, cooperation on science, language diplomas and indigenous languages; and cooperation by both academic institutions and businesses within the EU (Recommendations 2015: 57).

The detailed recommendations, of which there are 108, are divided into the categories of politics, the economy, cooperation, and the regional and multilateral context. The political recommendations include:

- maintaining a continuous political dialogue at a high level;
- implementing yearly consultations at the level of vice ministers or directors of the ministries of foreign affairs, alternately in Poland and Mexico;
- approving a yearly plan of meetings of the mechanism of political consultations, which should provide a basis for the development of bilateral relations in other areas;
- strengthening the parliamentary dialogue by establishing or reactivating the Polish-Mexican Friendship Group in the parliaments of both states, and by taking advantage of parliamentary relations in regional or multilateral forums such as the Inter-Parliamentary Union, the Euro-Latin American Parliamentary Assembly and the EU-Mexico Mixed Parliamentary Commission;
- exchanging experience within the scope of infrastructure, energy, innovation, health services and sustainable development;
- exchanging experience between the ministers of education of the two states.

The areas of possible cooperation mentioned include projects concerning the natural environment, farming, health care, water management, sanitation, energy and strengthening relations between societies through cultural events and scientific cooperation. In the regional and multilateral context, there is a mention of taking advantage of regional groups such as the PA and the Visegrad Group to reinforce bilateral and regional cooperation, and developing a multi-cultural dialogue in areas of mutual interest such as disarmament, sustainable development, human rights and democracy (Recommendations 2015: 58–61).

Towards a strategic partnership

A positive sign of the efforts being made to strengthen bilateral contacts at the highest level and of the political will to intensify Poland's relations with Mexico was the first-ever visit by a Polish president to Mexico on 22–25 April 2017, during which President Andrzej Duda met both his counterpart, Enrique Peña Neto, and the mayor of the capital city, Miguel Ángel Mancera, and took part in a ceremonial session of the Mexican Senate. Duda also inaugurated the Polish Investment and Trade Agency – the first such institution in Latin America and the Caribbean – and took part in a bilateral Economic Forum. The goal of the visit to Mexico was to support the Polish economy and Polish businesses interested in entering the Mexican market.

The presidents of both countries signed a joint declaration titled "Towards a strategic partnership between Poland and Mexico", which confirmed the long tradition of contacts between the two states, and emphasised that Mexico's position in the western hemisphere and Poland's role in the European Union and Central and Eastern Europe have beneficially affected the possibility of developing bilateral, regional and global cooperation between them. It also emphasised the benefits of cooperation within the UN and the OECD on such issues as human rights, reform of the UN, peacekeeping operations, disarmament, non-proliferation of weapons of mass destruction, sustainable development, climate change and projects concerning Central America and the Caribbean.

The document is divided into three parts: political dialogue; bilateral trade and investments; and cooperation on education, culture and technology. Strengthening economic ties is recognised as an essential condition for deepening bilateral relations. Also signed was a series of understandings aimed at intensifying cooperation, including: an executive programme to the agreement on cooperation in the fields of education and culture between the government of the Republic of Poland and the United States of Mexico for the years 2017–2021; a letter of intent by the minister of internal affairs and administration of the Republic of Poland and the minister of administration of the United States of Mexico on cooperation within the scope of police and border services training; agreements between the minister of sport and tourism of the Republic of Poland and the National Commission on physical culture and sport of the

United States of Mexico on cooperation in the field of sport; an understanding on a partnership between PTAK WARSAW EXPO and the Mexican Tourism Promotion Council; and an understanding between the Polish Space Agency (POLSA) and the Mexican Space Agency (Agencia Espacial Mexicana, AEM) on technical and scientific cooperation on space research and using outer space for peaceful purposes. During a speech at the Polish-Mexican Economic Forum, President Andrzej Duda emphasised that Poland is particularly interested in deepening cooperation in such areas as electromobility, information and communication technologies, the green economy, pharmacology and biotechnology, and investments (Declaración Conjunta "Hacia una relación estratégica entre México y Polonia").

***

The development of political contacts between Poland and Mexico was not favoured by their historical experience, geographical remoteness or political choices. Yet, apart from a number of short-lived episodes, relations between them did develop. Even during the Cold War, when the two countries found themselves on opposite sides of the Iron Curtain, they tried to avoid controversial subjects, limiting direct contacts to official visits confirming the good state of relations between them but not contributing to the development of any genuine partnership. In a certain sense, the cultural sphere provided a kind of compensation for those shallow political relations – an area in which the foundations of economic cooperation could gradually be laid without problems.

Mexico, like the rest of Latin America, was not considered a priority partner in Poland's foreign policy. After 1989, as well, it took a long time for Polish decision-makers, who were primarily focused on the country's close vicinity, to become aware of the need to intensify contacts with non-European countries. One can say that it was only Poland's accession to the European Union that provided an impulse to develop relations with the countries of Latin America, though these continued to take a back seat to other non-European regions such as Asia, the Middle East and Africa.

The ongoing process of globalisation means, however, that one ignores the growing importance of developing countries at one's peril. Mexico has a complex regional identity. By nature it is both North American (geographically, and more and more politically and economically as well) and Latin American (culturally, religiously, linguistically), and forms a bridge between the two American continents. Politicians and researchers often speak of it as a hinge country or bridge country, a nation of double regional membership or a bi-regional nation, or even as a nation of multiple belongings. It is the second-largest Latin American economy (after Brazil) and a country that is striving to play an increasingly important role as a global player. Mexico is open to international cooperation, and is not only maintaining and expanding old alliances, but is also looking for new partners such as Poland and Portugal (de Icaza 2018: 29). Mexico's international activation, which coincides with Poland's gradual diversification of its political and economic partners, is conducive to establishing close contacts and turning the formal frameworks for bilateral relations created over the years into genuine cooperation. Through its strategic partnership, Poland not only gains an important partner, especially within multilateral organisations, but also an advocate of its interests throughout the region of Latin America and the Caribbean, where it is increasingly active.

Poland is aware that at present it is not making full use of the potential of its relations with Mexico. Poland also perceives Mexico's growing position at the regional and global levels, meaning that Mexico is gradually emerging as a country that is important both within Latin America and, more broadly, outside Europe. The first-ever visit by a Polish president to Mexico, that was made by President Andrzej Duda in 2017, not only reflected the evolution of how Mexico is perceived by Polish decision-makers, but also initiated a new opening in the bilateral relations between the two states. There is hope that, in the years to come, it will be possible to build on the foundations already laid and create a real partnership – especially in view of the fact that the two countries have much to offer each other.

II Polish-Mexican economic relations

History of economic relations between Poland and Mexico

Although Poland and Mexico have sometimes had considerably different views on political issues, their relations have usually been fairly smooth, especially in that they were cemented by economic contacts that were for the most part developing steadily. As Tadeusz Łepkowski writes, "one could even say that there were two main causes why Poland established consular and diplomatic ties with Mexico: firstly, in order to organise and develop trade exchange, and secondly, to protect Polish citizens who were settling in Mexico in the 1920s" (Łepkowski 1980: 108).

The history of the economic relations between Poland and Mexico, however, goes back much further than this. Even during the colonial period, ships sailing between ports in Mexico were built from Polish wood and sealed with Polish pitch. During periods of drought, Mexico imported Polish grain, while products made of Mexican silver reached Poland, mainly through Spain and Holland. Contacts became closer in the 19th century, when Poland began importing cotton from Mexico and sending Polish industrial goods there (Smyk, Grudziński 2007: 92).

Polish-Mexican trade exchange began in 1924, and can be divided into two phases up to the outbreak of the World War II. Up to 1932, that exchange was mainly symbolic. During the 1920s, a decade marked by a global crisis, mutual trading was irregular, with Poland making use of both the inconvenient intermediary of third countries and of help from Mexican merchants of Polish-Jewish origin associated with the Polish Trade Agency (Agencia Comercial Polaca)[7]. Poland's main exports were textiles, vodka, zinc sheeting, plywood and cigarette paper. Mexico, in turn, exported vegetable fibre, zinc, copper, cotton and coffee to Poland (Łepkowski 1980: 112). Despite diplomatic efforts on both sides, as a result of an intensification in protectionist measures brought on by

---

7   The precursor of the Agencia Comercial Polaca was the Agencia Comercial del Consulado General de Polonia, active at the Polish Consulate up to 1929. Its main purpose was to provide information on Poland's economic offer, as well as direct assistance in establishing direct contacts with Polish businesses. See Krzysztof Smolana, Polska i Meksyk na przestrzeni dziejów widziane z perspektywy misji dyplomatycznej, Embajada de República de Polonia en México, Instituto Matías Romero, Secretaría de Relaciones Exteriores de México, México 2018, p. 268–269.

Tab. 1: Value of trade exchange between Mexico and Poland, 1935–1939 (in pesos). Source: Krzysztof Smolana, Polska i Meksyk na przestrzeni dziejów…, op. cit., p. 269

Year	Exports from Poland to Mexico	Exports from Mexico to Poland	Balance for Poland
1935	601,023	69,987	531,136
1936	678,451	1,263,377	-594,926
1937	1,800,749	984,702	816,047
1938	1,993,852	923,573	1,070,279
1939	984,496	710,623	273,873

the Great Depression, and because of disputes over customs duties and the most-favoured-nation clause, no Polish-Mexican treaty on friendship, trade and shipping was concluded (Łepkowski 1980: 115). At that time, Mexico came in fourth place – after Argentina, Brazil and Chile – on the list of Poland's Latin American economic partners (Łepkowski 1980: 118). Beginning in 1933, a post-crisis period of increasing bilateral economic relations began, though this did not actually result in a significant intensification of trade exchange. Among the beneficial effects of those relations was that Poland twice achieved a positive trade balance (in 1937 and 1938), and gradually resigned from using the services of middlemen in trade; on the other hand, Mexico dropped to sixth place among Poland's Latin American partners. In the years 1933–1938, Poland's trade with Mexico amounted to 19.9 million zlotys, whereas with Argentina it was 242.7 million, with Brazil 127.9 million, with Colombia 41.2 million, with Chile 30.5 million and with Uruguay 23.4 million (Łepkowski 1980: 119–120). There was no coherent, consistent trade policy in either country. Polish exports mainly comprised paraffin, plywood (in the 1930s Poland supplied more than half of Mexico's demand for this product), cellulose, brewer's barley and hops, potato flour, enamelled dishes, furniture and tissue paper. From Mexico, Poland mainly imported raw materials. Before World War II, Polish-Mexican trade relations developed unusually slowly. Beginning in 1934, Mexico's strategy was to replace imports with industrialisation in order to boost own production and restrict external purchases. During the presidency of Lázaro Cárdenas (1934–1940), the process of industrialising Mexico was begun, and the economic policy of the state aimed at promoting own production and restricting imports, which had an adverse effect on trade with Poland.

      Help in deepening trade contacts was to be provided by, for example, the Polish-Latin American Chamber of Commerce (Cámara de Comercio

Polono-Latino-Americana) established in Warsaw in the middle of the 1920s. Yet the organization did not meet with much interest on the part of the Polish government, and played only a small role in the development of trade between Poland and Mexico. In this period, there was a preference for using the services and help of the Polish diaspora in Mexico. At Polonia's initiative, and with the support of Polish members of parliament, in 1935 Compañía Mercantil Transmaritima (laterTransmar S.A.) was created; it became actively engaged in the development of Polish-Mexican trade exchange. Also in 1935, the Gulf Gdynia Line was founded, which made it possible to create trade transport infrastructure and to reduce the costs of trading, which up to then had gone through much more expensive American ports. One can agree, then, with Tadeusz Łepkowski that, up to World War II, Polish-Mexican trade relations were limited to trade exchange, and were not very significant for the economies of either Poland or Mexico (Łepkowski 1980: 128).

During the World War II, Polonia circles in Mexico also engaged in economic cooperation. On 18 February 1942, the Polish Chamber of Trade Exchange in Mexico was established under the direction of Jan Skoryna. The goal of the institution was to prepare the Mexican market for cooperation with post-War Poland and to help Polish emigrants to Mexico find means of making a living (Smolana 2018: 293).

After the end of the war, Mexico was the second Latin American country (after Argentina) with which the Polish People's Republic established trade contacts. In 1948, a Polish trade office was opened, though trade exchange remained at a minimal level and was not regulated by any agreements. As Radosław Smyk and Adam Grudziński write: "In 1950, statistics did not record any imports from Mexico to Poland, while Polish exports were estimated at only 100,000 UDS" (Smyk, Grudziński 2007: 93).

Polish-Mexican economic relations after 1945

During the Cold War, bilateral relations were limited to courtesy visits and cultural contacts. It is true that from 28 September to 2 October 1950, a Mexican economic mission came to Poland to test the feasibility of signing a trade agreement, but that visit did not lead to any concrete results (Smolana 2018: 335). At that time, Mexico was not engaged in any intensive trade with social states; its trade exchange with the entire Eastern bloc did not exceed 1% of its total trade turnover (Smyk, Grudziński 2007: 89). The atmosphere became more conducive to a deepening of economic cooperation only in the 1960s. In 1963, a trade agreement was signed that contained a favoured-nation clause within the scope of trade and shipping that facilitated tender processes; however, that agreement never entered into force. An understanding was also approved between Nacional Financiera S.A. and Bank Handlowy S.A. on establishing banking procedures for the investment financing of shipments of goods (Smolana 2018: 339). Symbolic of such positive changes was a contract in 1968 for the construction of two cargo ships for Mexico – the Maya and the Aztec. These were the first ships exported by a Polish shipyard to the West. From the end of the 1960s, there was a systematic, though gradual, increase in trade exchange between Poland and Mexico, though certain fluctuations in turnover were also noted. These were caused mainly by large, one-off transactions that increased turnover even several fold statistically and were followed by a fall back down to normal levels. This was the case in 1975–1976, when Mexico bought six fishing trawlers having a total value of about 15 million USD, and in 1979, when a significant increase in turnover was caused by a large, one-off purchase of coffee from Mexico (Smyk, Grudziński 2007: 94). Trade exchange between the two states, though, was marginal, and Mexico's turnover with Poland did not exceed 0.3% of its total turnover and Poland's with Mexico – 0.2% (Smyk, Grudziński 2007: 94).

The development of economic relations was hampered by the difficult years of the 1980s, which brought political and economic changes for Poland that ultimately led to the collapse of the communist system, while in Mexico a serious economic crisis initiated a series of internal transformations. There was growth in trade exchange only after 1989. This was monocultural to a large extent, based on farming and food products, and was often dependent on one-off sales of such products as, for example, rape, casein and powdered milk (Smyk, Grudziński 2007: 94). Prevailing difficult economic conditions meant that from the beginning of the 1990s, both states began looking for new areas to cooperate. As a result, on 11 October 1990, an agreement on air traffic was signed, and on 14 May 2004 an agreement on cooperation in the field of tourism (Smolana 2018: 349). During a visit by Prime Minister Jerzy Buzek to Mexico in 1998, a convention on the avoidance of double taxation and an agreement on visa-free movement were also signed, which greatly facilitated direct contacts. Towards the end of the 1990s, the structure of export goods included chemicals, metallurgical products, mechanical devices and textile products. There was also a decline in imports; these consisted mainly of tropical fruits (bananas), which were connected with Poland's introduction of a system of preferential duty rates that did not cover Mexico (Smyk, Grudziński 2007: 95). This downward trend in turnover was slowed and gradually turned around at the beginning of the 21st century, although trade exchange continued to be unduly small in relation to the two countries' potential.

Tab. 2: Poland's trade balance with Mexico, 1998–2004, in thousands of USD. Source: Central Statistical Office yearbooks for the years 1999–2005, after: R. Smyk, A. Grudziński, Stosunki gospodarcze…, op. cit., p. 96

Year	Exports to Mexico	Imports from Mexico	Trade turnover	Balance
1998	19,761	32,936	52,697	-13,175
1999	38,203	42,823	81,026	-4,620
2000	44,946	56,431	101,377	-11,485
2001	104,381	84,097	188,478	20,284
2002	52,964	97,141	150,105	-44,172
2003	76,546	124,691	201,237	-48,145
2004	89,269	120,167	209,436	-30,898

Given their distance from Poland, the states of Latin America were not traditionally perceived as important trade partners. They were deemed as such only once, by the authorities of the Polish People's Republic in 1980 (Gocłowska-Bolek 2009: 33). The economic transformation that began in 1989 led to a breakdown in economic exchange. There was a departure from exchange settlements based on international agreements, and foreign trade was adapted to the needs of the free market (Gawrycki 2010: 434). Only Poland's accession to the EU caused a certain, though small, revitalisation of economic relations. The Latin American markets would seem to be an attractive direction for investment by Polish investors because of their high complementarity, yet there is a lack of appropriate assistance programmes for exporters.

In 2004, Vicente Fox visited Poland. This was the first visit to Poland by a Mexican president since 1963. Fox was accompanied by a delegation of representatives of Mexican business. The formal and legal effect of the trip was an agreement on cooperation in the field of tourism. Intensified activities were announced to determine fields and directions for deepening economic relations. Also, a Polish-Mexican group of experts from the field of the economy was established in order to conduct periodic reviews of the state of bilateral relations in this aspect, and to identify promising sectors of the economy in which opportunities existed for increasing trade exchange (Żurawska 2014: 220–221). Moreover, in 2004, a cooperation agreement was concluded between the National Chamber of Commerce (KIG) and the Mexican Foreign Trade Council (Concejo Empresial Mexicano de Comercio Exterior, COMCE).

Mexico's growing importance to the economic policy of Poland is also attested to by the fact that it was counted among Poland's priority states from the Latin

American and the Caribbean region in a document from 2004 titled "Strategy of the Republic of Poland in relation to non-European developing nations", with which countries the strategy posited an intensification of political relations and economic cooperation: "in relation to priority states, Poland's activities should focus on an intensive reinforcement of political and economic ties, promotional and informational activities, the formation of cooperation on the principle of partner relationships, the use of numerous multifaceted mechanisms, and increased activity in favour of exports of Polish investments" (Strategia 2004: 6). These areas of cooperation were treated as most important in relation to Mexico as well in a report titled "Challenges for the Foreign Policy of the Republic of Poland in respect of Latin America and the Caribbean 2015–2020 and after 2020", published under the auspices of the America Department of the Ministry of Foreign Affairs of the Republic of Poland in 2015. Among the potential areas of cooperation mentioned were the energy and exploration sector; the auto, shipyard and green technologies industries; IT and communications technologies; transport; the farming and food industry; medical equipment; aeronautics; cosmetics; and furniture.

Mexico found itself among four Latin American countries (alongside Chile, Colombia and Peru) targeted by Polish diplomatic activities in the years 2015–2016. At that time, work was begun on establishing a strong dialogue with Mexico, which culminated in a way when Poland obtained observer status in the PA. The PA is a very important bloc in terms of both the economic and demographic contexts. The member states of the PA, that is, Chile, Colombia, Mexico and Peru, together constitute the eighth largest economy and the eighth largest exporting power in the world. They are responsible for 37% of GDP in Latin America and the Caribbean, 52% of total trade and 45% of foreign direct investments. At the same time, with more than 225 million inhabitants with an average per capita GDP of more than 16,000 USD, they constitute an enormous market and a significant force in terms of both an educated workforce and potential consumers[8].

In 2016, Poland's trade turnover with Latin America and the Caribbean amounted to 5.73 billion USD, including exports of 1.99 billion USD and imports of 3.74 billion USD. The share of turnover with Latin America and the Caribbean in the total trade turnover of Poland was, in particular years: in 2016 – 1.4%, in 2015 – 1.8%, where year-on-year Poland has noted a negative trade balance with

---

8   For more, see Alianza del Pacífico. El poder de la integración, https://alianzapacifico. net/en/what-is-the-pacific-alliance/ (accessed: 24.07.2018).

the region of more than 1.5 billion USD. The main recipients of Polish exports in 2016 were Mexico (531 million USD), Brazil (363 million USD), the Bahamas (337 million USD), Antigua and Barbuda (185 million USD), Colombia (98 million USD), Chile (95 million USD), Argentina (79 million USD), Panama (57 million USD), Peru (56 million USD) and Cuba (48 million USD). The share of Latin America and the Caribbean in Poland's foreign trade is about 1.5%. The main goods exported by Poland to the region are, apart from ships (mainly for renovation): electrical and electronic equipment, machines and mechanical devices, cars, fuels, mineral oils, and fertilizers. Polish imports include, apart from ships (mainly for renovation): feed components (mainly soy cakes), fruits and nuts, airplanes and metal ores. The value of Polish direct investments in Latin American countries at the end of 2016 was 103.5 million USD (including 65.4 million USD in Central America, and 38.1 million USD in South America). Polish businesses increasingly see the Latin American markets as potential customers for goods and services from the building, energy, transport, mining, shipyard, arms, aviation and technologies sectors.

Bilateral cooperation after 1989

The general shape of Polish-Mexican economic and trade relations is set by the Agreement on Economic Partnership, Policy Coordination and Cooperation between Mexico and the European Union of 1997 – the Global Agreement (current undergoing negotiations on being updated and modernised). Its trade section (Tratado de Libre Comercio entre la Unión Europea y México, TLCUEM) entered into force on 1 July 2000. Since 2014, Mexico, as a country having a high average income, ceased to be covered by the existing formula for development cooperation with the EU as part of the Development Cooperation Instrument (DCI). The new formula for cooperation is based on a Partnership Instrument (PI), within which partners should strive to combat the effects of climate change, to increase trade exchange by using the potential of the TLCUEM and to implement the provisions of sectoral dialogues (environmental protection, science and technology, education, human rights and security). On the issue of trade liberalisation, both parties emphasise the need for a broad, comprehensive modernisation of the TLCUEM and to ensure its cohesion with other free trade agreements concluded or currently being negotiated between Mexico and the EU. In May 2016, the EU Council authorised the European Commission to begin negotiations with Mexico on the modernisation of the Global Agreement, including the Free Trade Agreement (FTA). Those negotiations encompass, among other items, trade in agricultural goods, including the elimination of customs duty;

rules of origin; market protection instruments; copyright protection; and geographical designations. In April 2018, the parties achieved a preliminary understanding on an agreement that is to replace the understanding in the year 2000.

In addition, the following agreements have been signed between Poland and Mexico within the scope of economic relations:

- a Convention between the Government of the Republic of Poland and the Government of the United States of Mexico on avoiding double taxation and preventing tax evasion within the scope of income tax of 30 November 1998. It came into force in 2003, and remains so until it is terminated by one of its signatories;
- an Agreement on Cooperation in the field of science and technology between the Government of the Republic of Poland and the Government of the United States of Mexico of 30 November 1998. Its purpose is to support, develop and facilitate joint research and development activities in the fields of science and technology. The agreement foresees, among other things, cooperation between research centres and research and technology institutions; the joint implementation of project of common interest; the organisation of scientific visits and exchanges, scientific training; joint research; the organisation of scientific seminars, conferences, symposiums and workshops; exchanges of experience; and studies on best practices within the scope of science and technology policy;
- an Agreement between the Government of the Republic of Poland and the Government of the United States of Mexico on cooperation in the field of tourism of 14 May 2004, which entered into force in 2005. Its goals are: to create conditions for the development and reinforcement of cooperation between Polish and Mexican international tourism organisations; to support the organisation of congresses, symposiums, exhibitions and other events conducive to the development of tourism; and to simplify border and customs formalities.

During his visit to Mexico in April 2017, President Andrzej Duda signed a series of bilateral understands on economic cooperation, including:

- a declaration on mutual cooperation between the Polish Ministry of Development and the Mexican Ministry of Economy (Secretaría de Economía);
- a memorandum of understanding (MoU) between the Polish Trade Investment Agency (PAIH) and the Mexican agency for promoting trade and investment, ProMéxico;

- a memorandum of understanding (MoU) in the area of export credits between Bank Gospodarstwa Krajowego (BGK) and the Mexican National Credit Society (Bancomext);
- a memorandum of understanding (MoU) in the area of export credits between the Export Credit Insurance Corporation (KUKE) and Bancomext;
- an agreement on technical and scientific cooperation within the scope of space research and the use of outer space for peaceful purposes between the Polish Space Agency (POLSA) and the Mexican Space Agency (Agencia Espacial Mexican, AEM);
- an extension of the cooperation agreement concluded in 2004 between the National Chamber of Commerce (KIG) and the Mexican Foreign Trade Council (Concejo Empresial Mexicano de Comercio Exterior, COMCE). Within COMCE, a Polish-Mexican Enterprise Committee function whose tasks are to support cooperation between Polish and Mexican companies and to further develop mutual economic relations;
- a partnership understanding between the Mexican Tourism Promotion Council (Consejo de Promoción Turística de México, CPTM) and PTAK Warsaw Expo.

The visit was an element of economic diplomacy, treated by President Duda as one of the priorities of Poland's foreign policy and made in order to increase opportunities for economic expansion and growth of the Polish economy, and to find new business partners in countries beyond the closest circle of Polish interests. During the visit, President Duda inaugurated the activities of the Foreign Trade Office of the Polish Investment and Trade Agency (PAIH) in Mexico City, the first such Polish representation in the Latin America and the Caribbean region. The business mission accompanying the president comprised representatives of financial institutions and companies from the automotive, food, chemical, aviation, defence, IT and energy sectors, as well as producers of medical equipment and furniture. President Duda also took part in a bilateral Economic Forum.

A joint declaration was signed, titled "Towards a strategic partnership between Poland and Mexico", which announced efforts to deepen bilateral cooperation in three main areas: political dialogue; bilateral trade and investment; and education, culture and technology. The document also encourages a strengthening of economic ties as a prerequisite for deepening bilateral relations, and emphasises Poland's support for renegotiating the Global Agreement between Mexico and the European Union. President Duda drew attention to the fact that Poland considers Mexico as a priority non-European trade partner. A joint declaration was also signed on cooperation aimed at establishing a High Level Working Party for Economic Matters (Grupo de Trabajo de Alto Nivel de Asuntos Económicos) between the Mexican Secretaría de Economia and the Polish Ministries of Investment and Development and Finance (Declaración Conjunta "Hacia una relación estratégica entre México y Polonia"). The visit gave a new impulse to intensify bilateral relations, and confirmed a "new opening" in Polish-Mexican relations and Mexico's growing importance in Polish foreign policy.

The actions taken to develop bilateral economic cooperation also included a seminar, "Opportunities for Polish businesses in Mexico", organized in April 2016 by the Investor Services and Foreign Cooperation Office of Łódź City Hall and the Mexican embassy in Poland, and a trade and investment seminar held in June 2012 under the patronage of the PAIH and ProMexico in cooperation with the Mexican embassy. From 30 September to 4 October of the same year, a series of economic promotional projects was run under the name "Polish Days in Mexico", combined with an official visit by a Polish government delegation headed by Undersecretary of State at the Ministry of Foreign Affairs, Beata Stelmach. The delegation was accompanied by a Polish business mission representing the exploration, pharmaceutical, transport, green technology, food, cosmetics and metallurgy sectors. The programme for the Polish Days covered projects of an economic, political or cultural nature, including a conference on prospects for growth in the oil and shale gas sectors; a Polish-Mexican economic forum titled "Poland. Gate to Europe"; and the inauguration of the Cervantino Festival in Guanajuato, of which Poland was one of the honorary guests. The Polish delegation also attended a series of bilateral meetings, including at the Ministry of Energy and the Ministry of Economy. A memorandum on cooperation between ProMexico and PAIiZ was also signed.

Programmes for promoting the Polish economy on the Mexican market are also run using EU funds, especially since Mexico again qualified as one of the five most promising global markets for an expansion of Polish trade and investments (alongside Algeria, India, Iran and Vietnam)[9]. This made it possible to cover Mexico by a special promotional programme to be implemented in the years

---

9   Mexico was deemed a promising market (along with Algeria, Brazil, Canada, Kazachstan, Turkey and the United Arab Emirates) for the first time in 2013. This resulted in it being covered by a special promotional programme financed out of EU funds within the Innovative Economy Operational Programme. In Mexico, that programme was implemented in 2014. Polish entrepreneurs can also take advantage of a promotional programme for the most promising branches of the Polish economy under the project "Go to Brand" offered by the Polish Business Development Agency (PARP).

2017–2019, to create a Foreign Trade Office within the PAIH, and for the Polish Ministry of Development and Finance and the Mexican Ministry of Economy to sign a memorandum of understanding laying out, among other items, a mechanism for regular bilateral consultations (Note 2017: 8).

Foreign trade

Mexico is among Poland's most important partners in the Latin America and the Caribbean region, not only in terms of the leading role it plays in intra-American relations in the international arena, but also because of the more than 80-year tradition of diplomatic relations between the two countries. Mexico is Poland's third-largest trade partner in Latin America, and its second-largest export market in the region for Polish products. Yet economic cooperation and trade exchange between Poland and Mexico does not live up to the potential and capabilities of the two states. Foreign trade with Mexico is mainly directed towards cooperation within North American Free Trade Agreement (NAFTA), while Mexico's turnover with the countries of Central Europe, including Poland, continues to be only a marginal part of its trade exchange. Mexico, however, views Poland as a country that can facilitate its entry onto other European markets.

In terms of turnover, Mexico is Poland's third-largest partner in Latin America, after Brazil and Argentina, but on the global scale occupies only 46th place. Mexico's share in Poland's trade exchange with Latin America is at a level of 13%[10]. In the years 2002–2008, Poland's trade turnover with Mexico featured steady growth in both imports and exports. In 2009, as a result of the global economic crisis, there was a slump in mutual trade, but in 2010, the trade exchange between Poland and Mexico recovered its previous growth rate.

According to date from the Polish Ministry of Economy, in 2011 trade turnover amounted to 566 million EUR, and Poland noted a trade surplus with Mexico for the first time since 2002. In 2012, bilateral trade exchange continued to grow, reaching 651 million euros, including Polish exports to Mexico of 408.4 million and imports from Mexico of 242.6 million. The growth rate in trade turnover in 2011–2012 was 115% – Polish exports went up by 131% while imports fell slightly to 95%.

---

10 Ministry of Foreign Affairs of the Republic of Poland, Stosunki gospodarcze Polski z Meksykiem i Ameryką Środkową https://meksyk.msz.gov.pl/pl/wspolpraca_dwustronna/ekonomia/ambasada_rp_w_meksyku_340/ (accessed 27.06.2018).

Tab. 3: Polish-Mexican trade turnover (in million euros). Source: Stosunki gospodarcze Polski z Meksykiem i Ameryką Środkową, https://meksyk.msz.gov.pl/pl/wspolpraca_dwustronna/ekonomia/ambasada_rp_w_meksyku_340/?channel=www (accessed: 27.06.2018)

	2010	2011	2012	2013	2014	2015	2016
Trade turnover	564.3	792	910.5	894.8	917.4	1,084.9	962.4
Exports	267.4	432.4	566.3	523.7	496.9	589.4	478.5
Imports	296.8	359.6	344.2	371	420.5	495.5	483.9
Balance	-29.4	72.7	222.1	152.7	76.4	93.8	-11

In 2013, trade exchange continued to grow, reaching 665.5 million euros, including Polish exports to Mexico of 395.1 million and imports from Mexico of 270.4 million. The growth rate in trade turnover in 2012–2013 was 102% – Polish exports went down to 97% while imports climbed to 111.5%.

In 2014, trade turnover with Mexico was 913.1 million EUR – a continuation of the dynamic growth trend. Exports from Poland reached 497.8 million EUR, and imports 415.3 million. In 2014, Polish exports of processed food products to Mexico amounted to 9 million euros, which represented an average annual increase of 89% in the years 2010–2014. The growth rate in trade turnover in 2013–2014 was 102% – Polish exports at 95% and imports at 112%.

In 2015, trade turnover between Poland and Mexico increased by 31% along with a favourable increase for Poland of 36% – the highest value seen in the last decade. Unfortunately, this growth trend stopped, and by 2016 turnover had fallen by 11.3%, while imports exceeded exports, resulting in a negative trade turnover balance.

The main goods exported from Poland to Mexico include: mechanical and electrical devices for recording and playing back sound; parts for cars, vehicles, aircraft, sailing vessels and associated devices; products from non-precious metals; chemical and related products; artificial materials and products from those materials; and plant-derived products. The structure of Poland's imports from Mexico is similar to that of Poland's exports there: mechanical and electrical devices for recording and playing back sound; vehicles, aircraft, sailing vessels and associated devices; and products from non-precious metals.

In 2017, the value of Polish exports was 2,572,700,000 zlotys (602.4 million euros), and that of imports 2,575,800,000 zlotys (603.47 million euros), which means that the country's trade balance was practically even. Polish exports to Mexico mainly comprise machines; mechanical and electric devices; vehicles, airplanes, ships and other means of transport; and chemical products. Poland imports machines, vehicles, instruments and equipment[11].

Mutual investments

In 2004, the PAIiIZ noted the first Mexican investment in Poland worth over 1 million USD. The company Cemex bought two Polish cement plants and invested in related production (concrete plants, raw materials for the production of cement and concrete, logistics). At present, Cemex is among the leading domestic producers of cement, ready-mixed concrete and aggregates. In 2006, Nemak, which produces replacement parts for cars manufactured by the Mexican Alfa group, finalised a transaction for the purchase of the Polish TK Aluminium plant. That transaction was worth 71 million USD. In 2009, through its subsidiary Katcon, Bienes Turgon, a Mexican holding company active in the auto industry took control over the company Delphia, a producer of exhaust systems located in Błonie near Warsaw.

The main areas of Polish investments in Mexico are the car industry (an investment by the company Bury Sp. z o.o. in the State of Tlaxcala – car parts), cosmetics (the company Inglot) and Polish-Mexican travel agencies. In terms of investment size, Poland is in the 13th place among EU Member States. In 2016, 21 companies with Polish capital existed in Mexico, of which the majority were in Mexico City and the states of Tlaxcala, Baja California Sur, Veracruz, and Quintana Roo (according to Informator Ekonomiczny). The cumulative value of Polish investments in Mexico in the period 1999–2015 was 19.2 million USD, where the highest value was achieved in 2009 (11.6 million USD) (Recommendations 2016: 48). Those investments covered eight main sectors of the economy including: manufacturing (74%), trade and leasing of real estate (22%), tourism (2.9%) and trade (1.1%) (Note 2017: 3). The most promising directions for developing economic cooperation include the auto industry, electronics, agriculture and agricultural equipment, energy, construction and infrastructure, and aviation. During the ILA Air Show 2014 in Berlin, aviation groups from Monterrey and Dolina Lotnicza in Poland signed a letter of intent that marked the first step towards cooperation in the aviation industry on, among other things, exchanges of information on the organisation and

---

11 Aleksander Fedoruk, Meksyk bramą dla polskich towarów i inwestycji za oceanem, "Business Insider", 7 maja 2018, https://businessinsider.com.pl/firmy/ strategie/wymiana-handlowa-polska-meksyk-inwestycje-w-meksyku/vk44c45 (accessed: 27.06.2018).

missions of enterprises and exchanges of personnel. In 2017, PZL Mielec also conducted promotional displays in Mexico of its M28 turboprop passenger and transport aircraft (Note 2017: 3). There is also a lot of potential in tourism (in 2016 the number of Polish tourists to Mexico increased by almost 20% up to 31,000 people), food products, environmental technologies and the production of plastic packaging.

In 2016, the Ministries of Foreign Affairs of both countries, in cooperation with the private sector and academic institutions, approved a document titled "Recommendations on a strengthening of relations between Poland and Mexico", which emphasised the economic potential of the two states and opportunities for deepening bilateral cooperation. In 2015, Poland was in the 32nd place among Mexico's global trade partners, 9th among EU countries and first among Central European countries. Mexico, in turn, was Poland's 46th-biggest trading partner, 3rd in both North and South America (Recommendations 2016: 46–47). The Recommendations also emphasised the importance of both states as gateways to the regions of Central America and Central Europe. Economically, those sectors recognised as having particular significance for bilateral relations were: cars, electronics, energy, construction and infrastructure, aviation, tourism, food products, promotional fairs and exhibitions that could promote a revival of trade and business, environmental technologies and energy efficiency. In particular, within the economic sphere the Recommendations covered:

- opening economic promotion offices in both countries (a PAIH Foreign Office in Mexico was opened in 2017);
- creating alternative mechanisms for promoting trade and investment (e.g. in the form of a Polish-Mexican Economic Joint Commission) and joining global value chains;
- defining promising sectors, promoting them through economic missions, and taking part in business fairs and seminars;
- using a network of consulates headed by honorary consuls in order to analyse existing opportunities on specific local markets and mutually promote tourism;
- considering the possibility of creating a high-level group for promoting tourism, increasing the output of that industry and tourism traffic;
- starting up a dialogue among customs institutions aimed at concluding an understanding on cooperation that would facilitate bilateral trade exchange, taking account of the provisions of the trade pillar of the Global Agreement concluded between Mexico and the EU, as well as a dialogue among migration institutions to determine the feasibility of starting negotiations on the

relocation of, for example, businessmen and investors (Recommendations 2016: 58–59).

During the conference "A reinforced Polish-Mexican dialogue: a new opening in bilateral relations", which was held in September 2016 in Warsaw, the reasons for the small interest shown by Polish and Mexican companies in direct investments were discussed. The most important of these include insufficient knowledge about the other country; a lack of familiarity with the markets, their characteristics and needs; and stereotypes that impede the establishment of real cooperation. While it is true that, in the last decade, the scope of Polish-Mexican economic relations has grown, mutual trade exchange remains at a low level that does not reflect the two countries' potential. The lack of a long-term strategy for economic cooperation means that most actions taken to intensify bilateral relations are ad hoc in nature, and do not translate into a measurable increase in the significance of the two countries to each other and to their economic policies.

Poland seeks to establish close economic ties with Mexico through the PA, of which Mexico is a member, and to make good use of the observer status it gained there in 2015. In June 2017, the National Chamber of Commerce and the America Department of the Ministry of Foreign Affairs organised a seminar, "The PA – an economic challenge for Poland", on the opportunities that cooperation with PA countries provides for Polish businesses. The seminar was attended by diplomats from PA countries, professors whose research focuses on Latin America, officials of Polish administration, and entrepreneurs and academics involved in propagating and promoting cooperation between Poland and the Latin American market. The seminar was addressed mainly to business circles, and had two main themes: the internationalization of small and medium businesses, and innovativeness in business in terms of the needs of PA countries.

The PA (Chile, Peru, Colombia and Mexico) is currently the most pragmatic and promising economic group in Latin America. The EU has concluded free trade agreements with all of its members. Poland has had observer status at the PA since July 2015. Currently, about 50% of Poland's trade exchange with Latin America and the Caribbean is with PA member states. Poland conducts regular, lively political cooperation with all of them.

Mexico's membership in the PA ensures that in the "Strategy for sustainable development to 2020 (with a perspective up to 2030)" – a key document for Poland's mid-term and long-term economic policy approved by the Ministry of Investment and Development in February 2017 – Mexico is perceived as a promising market, especially in respect of the auto and aviation industries (SOR 2017: 139). Cooperation with the PA is one of the Polish government's priorities regarding Latin America, and half of Poland's trade turnover with the region is with the members of the alliance. As an observer in that group, Poland promotes cooperation in such areas as: the internationalisation of small and medium businesses, and innovation ("The PA – an economic challenge for Poland").

The importance of Mexico and, more broadly, Latin America, as alternative markets for the Polish and EU economies has grown since the economic crisis of 2008, when Latin America began to appear attractive as a way of diversifying destinations of Polish exports, particularly in the face of trade difficulties with Russia and Ukraine.

***

It is the economic perspective that dominates in Poland's foreign policy towards Latin America and the Caribbean, and also in its bilateral relations with particular states, including Mexico. Mexico is considered the world's 14th-largest economy, and its Gross Domestic Product (GDP) is 1.7% of world GDP. Its foreign trade produces 60% of its GDP, while its market – one of the most open in the world – ensures access to more than 110 million potential consumers. Mexico is also the only state with which the EU has both an association agreement and a strategic partnership (concluded in 2008). The purpose of the partnership, which is an expression of recognition of Mexico's growing role in the world, is to increase bilateral cooperation and coordinate activities at the multilateral level. One of the forms taken by the strategic partnership is EU-Mexico summits. These are complemented by a regular dialogue at the high level on such subjects as human rights, security, law enforcement, the economy, environmental protection and climate change. Apart from Europe, Mexico is also intensifying its contacts with other Latin American states, and is opening itself up to trade with the Asia and Pacific region, as seen in its membership in the PA.

Mexico is becoming increasingly active in terms of economic activity internationally. It is an active member of the WTO, the OECD, the International Monetary Fund, and the G20. At the same time, in connection with the renegotiation of the NAFTA agreement instigated by the USA, Mexico is opening itself up to cooperation with new partners, and is seeking to diversify its economic contacts. The economic diplomacy being conducted by President Andrzej Duda has similar goals. It would seem, then, that now is the time to tighten bilateral economic contacts. Existing trade between Poland and Mexico is at a level well below the capabilities of the two countries. Even with an awareness of its limited resources and means, Poland has an opportunity to change this negative trend. Certainly, this will require greater engagement on the part of both the Polish government and the private sector, as well as the creation of a long-term economic strategy and a more effective use of EU instruments.

III Polish-Mexican relations in the fields of culture and science

History of cultural and scientific relations between Poland and Mexico

During the Spanish conquest and the colonial era, knowledge in Poland about the New World was very limited. The first reports on the conquest of Mexico were brought to Poland by Jan Dandyszek – an envoy of the Polish King Sigismund Augustus to the court of Emperor Charles V from 1525 to 1533, who was a friend of Hernán Cortés, and corresponded directly with him.

Another early contact was that printing fonts from a printing house in Seville belonging to the family of Stanisław Polak were brought to Mexico by Bishop Juan de Zumárraga; they were used in the first-ever printing house in the Americas (Rycerz 2007: 53). During the Enlightenment, interest in Mexico and its history and culture grew in Poland. In the tragic fate of the aboriginal tribes conquered by Cortés, Poles saw an analogy with their own condition of having been torn apart by the partitioning powers.

With few exceptions, such as Karol Beneski, who remained in the service of Emperor Augustín de Iturbide, Poles took no part in the Mexican War of Independence (1810–1821), although they were involved – on various sides – during the French intervention in Mexico in the years 1862–1867. It is from this period that the first published memoirs of Polish soldiers derive, including those of Prince Stanisław Wodzicki (1844–1921) "With the Ulans of Emperor Maximilian to Mexico. Memoirs of an Officer" (Kraków 1931) and the diary of Konrad Niklewicz, "Memories of Mexico. Mexico during the Reign of Maximilian I" (Warsaw 1901). In the 19th century, numerous scientific expeditions and journeys took place that resulted in publications in Polish on the subjects of Mexican flora, fauna and geography. Among the best known are works by Antoni Stadnicki (1874–1906) – "In Both Hemispheres. Travel Impressions and Letters" (Kraków-Warsaw 1911), Witold Szyszłło (1881–1963) – Mexico (Warszaw 1912), and Emil Habdank Dunikowski (1855–1924) – "Mexico and Sketches from Travels through Latin America" (Lwów 1913) (Rycerz 2007: 55).

In the 19th century, the Polish press reported news from Mexico only rarely, but took a positive view of the reforms of Porfirio Díaz, emphasizing his contribution to the development of civilization in Mexico. An important event in Polish-Mexican cultural relations during this period was the reception given in

Mexico to the distinguished pianist Ignacy Paderewski, who visited the country while touring the USA. Much was made of Paderewski being a Pole. In the context of the lack of Polish statehood at that time, this was very significant politically, for it could be interpreted as Mexico unofficially supporting Poland's aspirations for independence. At the same time, the Mexican opposition took advantage of Paderewski's presence to criticise the "Porfiriato". In 1900, the front page of the newspaper "El hijo de el Ahuizote" featured a picture of the pianist titled "Porfiriowski": the text reminded people that since 1884 Paderewski had performed in Mexico four times already, and was preparing yet another tour, thus alluding to Mexico's many years of government under Porfirio Díaz, who was hanging on to power and seeking another term of office (Mexico and Poland. Centuries of Cultural Relations 2015)[12].

At that time, Polish perceptions of Mexico were largely based on stereotypes of Mexico as an exotic country with a mysterious culture that had become Christianised as a result of the Spanish conquest, and a country embroiled in internal conflict since gaining independence. The period of the Porfiriato (1877–2911) was seen as a time of order, reform and the development of the state, while perceptions of the Mexican Revolution (1910–1917) were grossly simplistic, shown as a time of violent political upheaval without taking account of the country's complicated economic and social conditions. After Poland won its own independence in 1918, interest in Mexico grew along with the religious conflict of the "Cristeros" in the years 1925–1929. The anti-clerical restrictions introduced by the Mexican authorities were generally presented in a negative light in Poland. At the same time, in Mexico knowledge about Poland was equally negligible, with the dominant stereotypes being that Poland was Catholic, poor and backward, though the Mexican elites were usually in favour of Polish aspirations for independence (Rycerz 2007: 56).

In general, though, cultural relations between the two states were extremely modest. They had limited knowledge about each other, while the great geographical distance between them and their cultural differences were not conducive to an intensification of contacts. Though diplomatic contacts were established in 1928, during the interbellum period there was little real development of cultural

---

12 In 1945, the Mexican sculptor Miguel Baquidano Camps created a statue of Ignacy Paderewski that was displayed in the Palace of Fine Arts in Mexico City. The authorities of the Polish People's Republic, however, did not agree to finance the work, and so the statute was finally unveiled only in 2001, in Paseo de la Reforma, one of the main thoroughfares of the capital.

relations – because of the two countries' different political systems, conditions on the international scene, the lack of any tradition of intellectual dialogue between them, and the Mexican Polonia, which was small and not very much engaged in maintaining relations with the Polish state (Rycerz 2007: 57). Yet, in some areas, certain successes were achieved. One example is in meterology. Research was conducted in Mexico by Polish scientists such as Dr Wacław Górczyński, the organiser of a local observatory, and Dr Zenon Lemański. Events popularizing knowledge about Poland were also organized by the Mexican authorities. For example, on 7 May 1931 an academic session on Poland was organized by the Academia Nacional de Historia y Geografía; such events were so sporadic, though, that they did not lead to any lasting closeness between the two states. As Tadeusz Łepkowski writes, "Polish-Mexican cultural relations were less than modest… Poland was set on maintaining lively cultural contacts with the countries of Western Europe that it valued highly – especially France – but had a feeling of superiority towards the achievements and products of science and the elitist, artistic culture in so-called exotic countries. Mexico, in turn, and specifically its intellectual elite – despite the revolution and its search for its own domestic, Indian cultural traditions – looked with admiration at Europe, and Western Europe in particular, and so, reflected in that light, at Poland. This certainly meant that Mexican initiatives at establishing cultural contacts with Poland, though rare, were more frequent than Polish initiatives" (Łepkowski 1980: 134–135). Diplomatic representatives of both states focused primarily on avoiding contentious issues[13].

Bilateral relations during the Cold War period

Although there was a cooling off in political relations during the Cold War; paradoxically, cultural contacts intensified, since these were treated as a kind of substitute for proper official relations. Many projects were organised in order to promote Polish culture in Mexico and Mexican culture in Poland. In Mexico, Polish diplomatic representatives engaged in cultural activities. In 1946, a series of performances that included Polish dances were put on (in Queretaro, Guanajuato and other locations) by an American ballet company under the direction of Prof. Waldeen van Falkenstein Brooke de Zet. In 1948, a Committee

---

13 In 1933, at a request from Mexico, screenings of the film "La Paloma" were stopped in Poland because of scenes that denigrated Mexico. In turn, in 1936 a similar request was sent to the Mexican Ministry of Foreign Affairs concerning a German film, "Polenblut". T. Łepkowski, Polska-Meksyk 1918–1939, Wrocław 1980, p. 87.

for the Year of Chopin Celebrations was constituted in Mexico City under the patronage of President Miguel Alemán, and in the following year, events around the centenary of the death of the Polish composer were organized. There were also a series of exhibitions, including Polish folk art – in 1950 in Morellia, and in 1951 in Veracruz – and another in 1955 to celebrate the work of Adam Mickiewicz on the centenary of his death (Smolana 2018: 336). Beginning in 1946, the Polish Press Agency began operating in Mexico City; Ryszard Kapuściński worked there from 1967 to 1972 (Smolana 2018: 336). Polish artists held classes in Mexican art schools, and the number of student exchanges and performances by artistic groups went up. There were also an increasing number of art exhibitions, and Poland was visited by two of the most eminent Mexican mural artists – Diego Rivera and David Alfaro Siqueiros.

In 1955, as a result of cooperation between Zachęta Central Art Exhibition Bureau and the National Front of Artists in Mexico, an exhibition of Mexican art was organised in Warsaw under the title Contemporary Painting and Graphics of the 16th–20th centuries. It included Frida Kahlo's "Wounded Table" (La Mesa Herida), with which an interesting story is connected: this painting, the largest of all of Kahlo's works, was created along with other well-known works of hers such as: "Two Fridas", "Dream" and "Self-portrait with Cropped Hair". In 1945, Kahlo sent "Wounded Table" to the State Museum of Western Art in Moscow, but in 1948, an order was issued for the dissolution of the museum. Thus, the picture no longer existed in museum collections and, known as a "work foreign to the principles of Soviet realistic art", was not shown publicly again until 1954. A year later, it was sent to Warsaw, where it was seen for the last time. The picture went missing just after the exhibition, and its whereabouts are still unknown.

The exhibition contained paintings and graphics from the 16th century to the present, and alongside works by Frida Kahlo were others by important 20th-century artists such as José Clemente Orozco, Diego Rivera and David Alfaro Siqueiros. There was also substantial documentation: photographs of murals, 50 art monographs, illustrated catalogues, periodicals and newspapers. The exhibition mainly featured artists engaged socially, many of whom were connected with communism. This display of Mexican art was met with an unusually lively reception, among both art critics and artists. It was covered by the most important Polish critics: Janusz Bogucki, Aleksander Jackowski, Jerzy Malina, Jerzy Olkiewicz, Konrad Winkler, Ignacy Witz, Andrzej Wróblewski and others. Yet what is most interesting, perhaps, is that one can find echoes of the Mexican exhibition in the works of artists who took part in the legendary exhibition at the Arsenal held several months later, which is considered the beginning of a thaw in Polish art.

In 1961, the National Museum in Warsaw also organised an exhibition titled "Treasures of Mexican Art from Pre-Columbian Times to the Present", which became one of the most important cultural events in Poland of the post-war period. In its two-month run, the exhibition was visited by about 200,000 people. It included works of art from the pre-Columbian era, the colonial period and modern times (Rycerz 2007: 58).

In Mexico, Polish art and culture was also promoted. On numerous occasions, the Museum of Modern Art in Mexico City organised exhibitions of Polish modern art, while an exhibition prepared by the Museum of the History of Textiles in Łódź was named by one Mexican critic as the artistic event of the year (Rycerz 2007: 59). Polish culture weeks were also organised, mainly in academic centres. Polish theatre also became popular in Mexico; in 1968, Jerzy Grotowski's renowned "Teatr Laboratorium" presented works during the Olympic games.

And, beginning in the 1960s, film contacts also gradually developed. In 1962, the Universidad Nacional Autónoma de México (UNAM) published a work by Nancy Cárdenas titled "Cine Polaco", which discussed the post-war history of Polish cinema. In 1976, a direct understanding on cooperation was signed between the Supreme Management of Cinema in Warsaw and the General Directorate for Radio, Television and Cinema of Mexico, pursuant to which the two states were able to become acquainted with each other's most important film achievements. A programme of student exchanges was initiated among art schools, thanks to which the Łódź Film School trained young Mexican directors such as Jan Manuel Torres, Raúl Zermeño and Lorenzo Arduengo (Rycerz 2007: 64). Since the year 2000, Mexican cinema has had a presence at the Latin American Cinema Festival in Warsaw, where it is very popular.

Literary contacts between Poland and Mexico have also intensified. Mexican literature began to be translated into Polish only after the World War II. In 1956, a translation of the 17th-century Mexican poetess Sor Juana Inés de la Cruz appeared in an anthology titled "Translations of Poetry from the Spanish", edited by Janusz Strasburger. And in the 1970s and 1980s, there was something of a boom in Poland of Latin American – including Mexican – literature. There were numerous translations of Mexican works into Polish. The most popular were the books of Carlos Fuentes, while "translations of Mexican literature, alongside Argentinian literature, are the best represented in Poland as regards writings from Latin American countries" (Rycerz 2007: 74).

Polish literature also remained unknown for a long time in Mexico. The first story by a Polish author to appear in Mexico was "The Rainbow" by Wanda Wasilewska, published in 1944 at the initiative of the Mexican left. Since then, the Polish author, most often published in Mexico, has been the Nobel Prize winner Henryk Sienkiewicz (Rycerz 2007: 71).

Because of the ideological differences that existed between the two states, direct contacts among artistic circles were limited. Among the small number of events of this type were visits by Carlos Fuentes, Fernando Benitez, Elena Poniatowska, Juan Rulfo and Sergio Fernandez. Mexico was visited by such Polish writers as Teodor Parnicki, Sławomir Mrożek and Edward Stachura.

An important event for the development of cultural relations was the signing of an Agreement on Cultural, Scientific and Technical Cooperation between the two countries on 24 July 1970 that covered the period 1974–1975. It initiated exchanges of specialists in those areas, and led to the development of four-year implementation programmes containing the main assumptions and goals of bilateral cooperation. Renewed several times, the agreement is the most important mechanism regulating Polish-Mexican cooperation within this scope.

Generally, however, though positive officially, cultural relations have been rather superficial and to a large extent have developed on their own, without much state support. There has been no long-term strategy for intensifying cooperation. A large role in promoting bilateral contacts has been played by Polonia circles in Mexico. For example, in 1973 in Chapultepec Park in Mexico City, a monument to Nicholas Copernicus was unveiled, designed by the Polish artist Mieczysław Walter. The ceremony turned into a real manifestation of Polish-Mexican friendship and cooperation (Moloeznik 2007: 136).

Cultural cooperation after 1989

The fall of communism in Poland and the political transformation that resulted lifted the odium of ideological limitations off Poland's foreign policy and enabled the country to pursue more independent activities internationally. Those changes also affected cultural policy, although at that time Poland was still focusing its efforts not on culture, but on expanding its legal and treaty basis with the countries of Latin America and the Caribbean.

Currently, bilateral cooperation in the field of culture and education takes place mainly on the basis of an Agreement on cooperation in the Field of Education and Culture between the Government of the Republic of Poland and the Government of the United States of Mexico, signed in Warsaw on 12 June 1997 (Journal of Laws of 1986 No. 37 item 184). Pursuant to the agreement, a joint Commission for Educational and Cultural Cooperation coordinated by the Ministry of Foreign Affairs in Poland and the Secretariat of Foreign Relations of Mexico was established; sessions of the commission are held alternately in

Warsaw and Mexico City at least once every four years, and it is one of the most important permanent instruments of bilateral cooperation. Its main tasks include:

a) evaluating and determining areas of priority in which particular projects for cooperation in the fields of education, culture, youth and sport are implemented;
b) preparing, approving and evaluating the implementation of executive programmes to the agreement;
c) supervising the proper implementation of the agreement and making recommendations deemed suitable to the parties (Journal of Laws of 1998: 2118–2119).

Apart from the 1970 Agreement on Cultural, Scientific and Technical Cooperation referred to above, other aspects of bilateral cooperation in the field of culture and science are regulated by an Agreement between the Minister of Sport and Tourism of the Republic of Poland and the National Commission for Physical Culture and Sport of the United States of Mexico on cooperation in the field of sport, signed in Mexico City on 24 April 2017.

The political transformation in Poland after 1989 marked a significant change in the scope of and opportunities for Polish foreign policy, but did not have a fundamental impact on intensifying cultural and scientific cooperation with Mexico. Latin America had to yield to the priority goals of Poland's international engagement, which were to normalise relations in Poland's immediate vicinity, to accede to the European Union, and to secure the state's vital interests by obtaining membership in NATO.

Nevertheless, cultural contacts were maintained at a respectable level, and even slowly developed. In 1990, a Mexican Friends of Chopin Society was developed, which also propagated the works of other Polish composers and artists. In 2003, at the Archive of New Files in Warsaw, there was an exhibition of documents dating from the archives of the Legation of the Second Republic in Mexico from 1921 to 1945 on the occasion of the 75th anniversary of the establishment of diplomatic contacts between Poland and Mexico (Rycerz 2007: 60).

At the same time, in Mexican universities, and especially art schools, many Polish artists and academics were working who have had a permanent impact on Mexican culture. Among the many names one could mention is a theatre director of Polish origin, Ludwik Margules (1933–2006). In 2003, he was awarded a State Prize in the field of art and culture for artistic achievement in the art of theatre and for training several generations of Mexican actors and directors (Rycerz 2007: 63).

The involvement of Mexican Polonia in the development of cultural contacts was also recognised by President Andrzej Duda who, during his visit to Mexico in 2017, emphasized that Poles has been co-creating Mexican culture for a long time. He awarded the singer Leszek Zawadka with the Knight's Cross of the Order of Polonia Restituta "for distinguished service to Polish culture, for achievements in artistic and creative work, and for activities for the benefit of the Polish community in Mexico". At the same time, the Knight's Cross of the Order of Merit of the Republic of Poland was awarded to: Marek Adamski, Luis Decelis Maciak, Hanna Kot-Arredondo, Józef Olechowski, Andrzej Rattinger-Aranda and dr Wiesław Skowroński. In turn, in a declaration titled "Towards a strategic partnership between Poland and Mexico", the presidents of both states expressed their support for a further strengthening of bilateral relations in the areas of political, economic, cultural, scientific, educations, sports and police cooperation.

The diplomatic outlets of both states are also involved in the implementation of cultural and scientific cooperation. In cooperation with the Polish embassy in Mexico, the Lech Hellwig Górzyński Prize is awarded by UNAM University for theatrical creativity to UNAM students, promoting the artistic growth of the young generation and popularising Polish theatre. In 2016, the embassy also donated its library collection to the Library of Mexico on the occasion of its 70th anniversary.

Mexican culture enjoys unflagging interest in Poland. As part of the celebrations of the 90th anniversary of the establishment of diplomatic relations between Poland and Mexico, a series of cultural events were held in both Poland and Mexico. Between 28 September 2017 and 21 January 2018, one of the largest cultural events ever in Polish-Mexican relations was held in Poznań – an exhibition titled "Frida Kahlo and Diego Rivera. The Polish Context". It displayed works by both artists from the collection of Jacques and Natasha Gelman, as well as works from private collections and museums in Mexico, Germany and Poland. The exhibition was the first and only exhibition in Poland on Kahlo and Rivera, and was enriched by a little-known Polish thread in the lives of the artists that, on the one hand, revealed their very close relations with authors of Polish origin (Bernice Kolko and Fanny Rabel)[14], and on the other hand documented the presence of pictures by Kahlo and Rivera and a graphic by Fanny Rabel at the

---

14 Bernice Kolko was a photographer who became close to Frida and Diego. It was also possible to view works by the artist Fanny Rabel (Fanny Rabinovich Duval), born in Poland, a student of Diego Rivera.

Exhibition of Mexican Art in Poland in 1955. The Kahlo-Rivera exhibition was part of a larger series of cultural events under the slogan "Frida Kahlo in Poland 2017", which included other exhibitions, film screenings, food demonstrations, theatre productions, lectures and courses in seven Polish cities. It is an example of cooperation among institutions, companies and artists from Mexico and Poland, and was the most important programme of Mexican culture to date in Poland. The key elements of the project included: an exhibition of photography "Frida and Diego. Long live life!", which featured works by great photographers such as Edward Weston, Manuel Álvarez Bravo and Guillermo Kahlo (Warsaw, Wrocław, Łódź, Kraków); a film series titled "Frida Kahlo's Mexico", co-organized by the National Cinematheque of Mexico and the National Film Archive in Warsaw (Warsaw, Wrocław, Łódź, Kraków); large-format multimedia presentations run by the well-known lecturer Gregorio Luke (Warsaw, Poznań, Łódź); the theatre play "Frida. Life Art Revolution" by the renowned director and actor Jakub Przebindowski (Warsaw); a course titled "Frida Kahlo's Mexico" run by experts from the National Autonomous University of Mexico (UNAM) (Warsaw); a food festival titled "Frida Kahlo's Kitchen" (Poznań, Kraków, Łódź); and a presentation of the Altar of the Dead dedicated to Frida Kahlo in the Ethnographic Museum in Warsaw in cooperation with the Museum of Folk Art of Mexico. The Mexican embassy in Poland also extended its honorary patronage to the publication of a book "*Frida Kahlo*", by the Poznań publishing house Widnokrąg.

In 2018, another exhibition was organized at the University of Warsaw that featured a fascimile edition of the Boturini Codex[15]. This was the first exhibition of the Aztec book in Poland, and was accompanied by a series of lectures with the participation of Mexican academic, including Dr María Castañeda de la Paz of the UNAM.

Also in 2018, in Mexico a week-long celebration of the 150th anniversary of the birth of Marie Curie-Skłodowska was held. In cooperation with the Instituto Matías Romero, the Polish embassy in Mexico published a bilingual book by Krzysztof Smolana titled "Polonia y México a lo largo de la historia: una perspectiva desde la misión diplomática polaca". There was also an exhibition of Polish poster artists at the Casa de Europa w San Miguel de Allende, Polish Culture Days (las Jornadas Culturales de Polonia) in Cuautitlán Izcalli,

---

15 The Boturini Codex, also known as the "Tira de la peregrinación", is an Aztec book 5.5 metres long and 20 cm wide folded into a harmonica. It tells the history of the Aztecs from their mythic beginnings, their exit from the mysterious land of Aztlan, to the founding of their capital in the Valley of Mexico.

and a Polish-Mexican music project, "Postcards (Postales)". A series of cinema events were held, including a retrospective of films by Andrzej Wajda along with some of his paintings. Other cultural events worth noting include a concert by the Amaedus Polish Radio Chamber Orchestra (la Orquesta de Cámara "Amadeus" de la Radio Polaca) at the Palacio de Bellas Artes in Mexico City and the exhibitions "On Poland (Sobre Polska) and Poland. Country of UNESCO World Heritage" (Polonia. País del patrimonio mundial de la UNESCO) at the Museo Regional de Cholula. In Poland, at the Roma Theatre in Warsaw a concert was held featuring the Mexican jazz artist Alex Mercado, along with a digital exhibition "Los senderos de la fascinación: Carteles de Polonia sobre México (1949–2010)" at the Poster Museum.

Scientific bilateral relations

Poland is a signatory to a number of scientific cooperation agreements with countries of Latin America, including Mexico. And since 1989, there has been observable growth in cooperation between Polish and Mexican universities, accompanied by an increase in the number of student exchanges between the two countries. Despite their geographic remoteness from each other and the resulting high costs of such exchanges, the number of Mexican students in Poland is about 50 per year, and is systematically growing, while Mexican comprise the second most numerous group among Latin American students in Poland (after Brazilians). Both states offer scholarships for students at different levels; these allow them to attend public universities, or take part in courses or scientific conferences.

One of the most important scientific events of the past two decades in Poland's relations with Latin American was organized in the year 2000 in Warsaw – the 50th International Congress of American Studies, attended by more than 1,800 representatives of academic circles, experts and representatives of the Polish authorities.

In November 2016, in cooperation with the Polish embassy in Mexico, a conference was held at the Universidad Autónoma de México (UNAM) which entitled Polish higher education and academic exchanges with universities in Poland, which presented the Polish higher education system, and the conditions for studying in Poland and cooperating with it academically. At the same university, celebrations of the 200th anniversary of the founding of the University of Warsaw were held, during which an exhibition was held at the Faculty of Architecture of the UNAM, titled "Two Centuries. A Good Beginning".

Poland and Mexico also cooperate in the field of technology, pursuant to an Agreement on Scientific and Technical Cooperation of 1998. Because to date no Joint Commission has been created thereunder, cooperation within this scope occurs directly between scientific bodies in the two countries. The Mexican International Cooperation Agency (Agencia Mexicana de Cooperación Internacional para el Desarrollo, Amexcid) defines sectors for possible cooperation; emphasis is placed on environmental protection, agriculture, health services, water and waste management, energy, science and technology, and tourism. In this context, the idea suggests itself of establishing contacts formally through a Joint Commission, or intensifying direct contacts between academics and representatives of the relevant institutions from the two states, including in the form of joint conferences and academic symposiums.

Potential areas in which measures can be taken are outlined in a document prepared by the two countries' Ministries of Foreign Affairs in 2016, "Recommendations on a strengthening of relations between Poland and Mexico", and one of those areas is training. Mexico, which has conducted a comprehensive educational reform in recent years, could benefit from Polish experience in this area. Mexico also perceives Poland as an important centre of music education, from which derive ideas for enabling Mexican students to take post-graduate studies in Polish conservatories, and for starting up a scholarship programme to finance such studies. It is also worth noting the continually growing interest in learning Spanish shown in Poland; promoting this could be used to popularise mutual knowledge and deepen cooperation within this scope, for example, by introducing Spanish language certificates issued by the Universidad Nacional Autónoma de México, or promoting the Polish language and Polish literature in Mexico. A good starting point could be the successful cooperation seen between Polish and Mexican institutions (University of Warsaw and the State Archive in Mexico and the Instituto de Docencia e Investigación Etnológica in Zacatecas), in cooperation with the University of Seville and the European Research Centre, in the form of a project promoting the Nahuatl language titled "Contacts between Europe and America: Multidisciplinary Studies on Cultural Influences in the New World over Time". The Recommendations also propose intensifying academic cooperation between Poland and Mexico under instruments offered by the European Union, including, for example, the Horizon 2020 programme for financing research and development (Recommendations 2016: 56–57).

Particular recommendations include cooperating on science and technology projects identified as displaying growth tendencies; strengthening relations between the two societies through cultural events organized with the support of the diplomatic missions and honorary consuls of the two states; disseminating information on available university scholarships and possibly increasing the scope of students exchanges; agreeing priority areas for science and technical cooperation within the procedure laid out in the provisions of the agreement on cooperation in the field of science and technology; promoting joint research projects to be implemented by scientific institutions in the two states; encouraging the participation of academics and experts from both states in events on science, technology and innovation organised by research centres and institutions of higher education in Poland and Mexico; striving to implement the "Chair of Mexico" project at the University of Warsaw; and promoting the Polish language in Mexico. There is also a recommendation to utilise sister cities in Poland and Mexico to promote the "Smart Cities" concept. (Recommendations 2016: 59–60).

Intensifying academic contacts between Poland and Mexico also takes place multilaterally, using instruments developed by the European Union. As an EU member, Poland has taken part in such projects as "Alfa Puentes", whose goal is to promote the idea of the Bologna process and the European Higher Education Area in the global context, including through the activities of the European Universities Association (EUA)[16]. The project focuses on: tightening cooperation among EU and Latin American university associations; modernising and coordinating systems of higher education in Latin American countries; supporting initiatives aimed at improving the quality of education; facilitating the recognition of diplomas and qualifications; and increasing academic mobility.

Opportunities and instruments for increasing cooperation concerning the internationalisation of science and higher education, UE-CELAC, was the subject of discussion during the 2nd Summit of Rectors' Conference Chairpersons of the European Union and Latin America and the Caribbean (II Cumbre de Presidentes de Consejos de Rectores de la Unión Europea – América Latina y el Caribe) held in Mexico in November 2016. Recommendations for further steps towards creating a common higher educational sphere between the EU and the Latin America and the Caribbean region were set out in a document approved at the end of the summit, "Agreement with Mexico". In 2018, an understanding was signed between the Polish Academic Schools' Rector's Conference (KRASP)

---

16 The EUA was formed in 2001 by a combination of the Association of European Universities and the Confederation of European Union Rectors' Conference. Its main purposes are to facilitate the process of educating students and to conduct research within the framework of the Bologna process. In 2018, the organisation had 850 members from 47 states.

and the National Association of Universities and Higher Education Institutions of Mexico (Asociación Nacional de Universidades e Instituciones de Educación Superior de México, ANUIES). At the same time, cooperation was deepened between the UNAM, Jagiellonian University (UJ) and the University of Warsaw (UW). One example of how the partnership between Mexico and Poland is already functioning is the "Chair of Mexico" programme of visiting professors at the UW, the goal of which is to ensure a suitable place for disseminating science and culture through meetings with guests from Mexico who specialise in the experimental sciences, social sciences and humanities[17].

Since 2018, Mexico has been one of 17 priority states covered by the I. Łukasiewicz Programme, whose goal is to support the social and economic development of developing states by raising their level of education and the professional qualifications of their citizens. Before studying in Poland, scholarship winners take part in an annual preparatory course run by Kraków University of Technology, Wrocław University of Technology or the University of Łódź. Beginning in 2019, the programme will make it possible for students to take 2nd-degree studies at universities supervised by the Ministry of Science and Higher Education, in such areas as the exact, natural and technical sciences, agriculture, forestry and veterinary science.

***

Despite differences in civilisation, language and historical experience, cultural relations between Poland and Mexico have constituted and continue to constitute an important element of their bilateral relations. They have withstood difficult moments in history, such as when for more than 100 years Poland was absent from the map of the world as a result of the Partitions, and when the world was divided ideologically during the period of the Cold War. They developed above those differences and, being uncontroversial, at times even constituted a substitute for official inter-state relations. What could not be conveyed openly in political contacts was expressed in art and in trans-Atlantic cultural relations, laying the foundation for mutual understanding between the two societies. From the Polish perspective, Mexican culture is colourful and exotic; it arouses curiosity and attracts throngs of admirers, as attested to by the enormous turnout during presentations of Mexican art in Poland and Poles' fascination with Latin

---

17 Ministerstwo Nauki i Szkolnictwa Wyższego, Polska zacieśnia współpracę z Meksykiem, https://www.nauka.gov.pl/ministerstwo/wspolpraca-z-zagranica/wspolpraca-dwustronna/mapa-swiata/meksyk/polska-zaciesnia-wspolprace-z-meksykiem.html (accessed: 30.07.2018).

American, including Mexican, literature. Cultural relations have broken down stereotypes that can hinder mutual understanding, and at times have increased Poles' inadequate knowledge about Mexico.

The political transformation that began in 1989, however, did not lead to a visible intensification of cultural relations between Poland and Mexico. Mexico and Latin America were not treated as a priority on the Polish foreign policy agenda. To a large extent, the breakthrough came only when Poland joined the EU in 2004. This gave Poland access to existing EU mechanisms for cooperation with Mexico, especially in the field of science. It also provided an impulse to intensify scientific contacts and establish academic cooperation among the most important centres in both countries. Given the recent educational reforms in Mexico, Poland can use this niche and share its experience within this scope. Support for innovation and joint projects could become important factors that not only benefit the development of the two states' economies, but also bring them closer together on the academic level, especially in the exact sciences.

Given the growing importance of soft power in international relations, Poland is also making increasing use of this in its foreign policy, putting greater emphasis on building up a positive image of the country. This concerns historical policy to a large extent, but it is also worth including activities that promote modern culture, music and film as those areas that have the biggest impact on propagating mutual understanding between societies. Today, this is facilitated by Poles' increasing knowledge of Spanish, their unflagging interest in Mexico and Mexico's attractiveness as a tourist destination.

At present, there is no overall strategy towards Mexico, or Latin America as a whole, in Polish policy. In respect of culture, there has been an intensification of events promoting cultural cooperation on the occasion of major anniversaries (e.g. of the establishment of Polish-Mexican diplomatic relations). Between such special occasions, however, that intensity is quite low, as is the level of the funding allocated to such events. Yet it seems that, in the long term, this area of cooperation may prove to be the one that is the least costly, the least controversial and that brings the most measurable benefits in terms of forging strong bonds between the peoples of Poland and Mexico.

IV Polonia in Polish-Mexican relations

At present, there are about 18–20 million Poles scattered around the world, of which only a small number live in Mexico. The Mexican Polonia[18], though, has a very interesting history and, properly directed, could be instrumental not only in increasing mutual understanding, but also in intensifying bilateral relations.

Geography and history have not been conducive to the development of such relations. During the time of the first Polish Republic, Mexico was a colony of Spain, and when Mexico was fighting for independence at the beginning of the 19th century, Poland was partitioned among Russia, Austro-Hungary and Prussia – wiped off the map of sovereign states for more than 100 years. At the time Poland regained its independence in 1918, Mexico was mired down in chaos and the consequences of the Mexican Revolution, which redefined the country's priorities internationally. Despite these objective difficulties, the two countries have a long history of direct contacts – and especially personal contacts.

First contacts

Poles appeared in Mexico after the failed November Uprising of 1830 and, despite being few in number, contributed much to the development of Mexico's cultural life[19]. One example of this is the surgeon Seweryn Gałęzowski, a Polish insurgent who lived in Mexico from 1834, and contributed to the establishment of the Faculty of Medicine at the University of Mexico City (Dobosiewicz, Rómmel 1977: 12). In the 1820s, Colonel Karol Bieniewski (Carlos Beneske de Beaufort) was Chief of Staff in the army of Augustín Iturbide. Another Polish emigrant, Konstanty Paweł Tarnawa-Malczewski (Constantino Pablo Tarnava de Malchesqui) attained the rank of general in the Mexican army, took part in the delineation of the new border between Mexico and the USA in 1948, and distinguished himself both as a poet (a pre-cursor of Romanticism) and as a lecturer at the Military Academy (Łepkowski 1970: 79). Other important figures in the Mexican army include Józef Tabaczyński, adjutant to President Ignacio

---

18 This term is used to describe people of Polish diaspora in the world, especially the old waves of migration started before the World War II.
19 The first Poles to set foot on Mexican soil were probably missionaries sent to Christianize the New World. Among the few names we know of is Jerzy Hostyński, who died in Mexico in 1686. Tadeusz Łepkowski, Polska-Meksyk 1918–1939, Zakład Narodowy im. Ossolińskich, Wrocław 1980, p. 11.

Comonfort (1855–1857) and later Benito Juárez (1857–1872), and Edward Adam Łusakowski, known in Mexico as Subikurski, who beat the French in an encounter in Sonora in 1853 and later became involved in organizing the cavalry for the constitutional governments (Smolana 2018: 224–225).

Mexico was also visited by Polish researchers and scholars. A participant in the November Uprising[20] and a well-known traveller, Edmund Strzelecki, went to Mexico twice, in 1834 and 1837, where he carried out meteorological and geological research (Słabczyński 1957: 68, 80–85). In the mid-19th century, the botanist Józef Warszewicz studied the flora of Mexico.

Yet some of the first Poles to appear in Mexico were neither refugees nor scientists. There were Polish soldiers who were in the ranks of the American army during its invasion of Mexico in 1846–1848, and during an intervention by the French for the purpose of establishing an empire headed by Maximilian Habsburg in 1861–1867. The French engagement took place after the defeat of another insurrection in Poland, known as the January Uprising (1863–1864), also aimed at restoring Poland's independence. Counting on support from Napoleon III for the Polish cause in the international area, many insurgents favoured the idea of French intervention. Arguments in favour of this were also provided by the anti-clerical politician Benito Juárez, who was seen by many Poles (most of whom are Catholics) as something of an "Anti-Christ" – though it must be admitted that few Poles were well informed about the real political situation in Mexico. Those Polish soldiers who took part in the Franco-Austrian intervention in Mexico can be divided roughly into four main categories: 1) those recruited by force into the Austrian ranks, mainly former insurgents of the November Uprising interned by the Austrians; 2) officers who volunteered, guided by conservative and clerical views; 3) political volunteers, convinced that only France's support could lead to Poland regaining its independence; 4) volunteer mercenaries, for whom the distant journey was to be a great adventure and a chance at getting rich (Łepkowski 1970: 82). It is hard to determine just how many Poles took part in the fighting in Mexico, though the figure most often used is about 2,000 (Łepkowski 1970: 83). Many of them, when they saw the huge differences in the conditions faced by the partisans and the invaders,

---

20 A Polish national uprising in the years 1830–1831 against the Russian Empire, one of the three partitioning powers. After the uprising was brutally suppressed by Russia, many insurgents and activists for Polish independence were forced to emigrate in order to avoid further repressions.

went over to Benito Juarez's side, for which some paid with their lives, executed as deserters. Several hundred Poles who were American citizens also joined groups of American volunteers who, after the end of the Civil War, went south to help those Mexicans fighting for the Republic. On a number of occasions, then, Poles in Mexico were engaged in a fratricidal war. After the collapse of the Second Empire and the execution of Maximilian Habsburg, most Polish soldiers returned to Europe, though some chose to emigrate to the United States, Cuba or a Central American state. A small group remained in Mexico, quickly became assimilated, and did not create any Polonia groups in the strict sense of the word (Smolana 2018: 239–240).

Apart from soldiers, another interesting group of Polish immigrants were miners, such as Henryk Henderson and Antoni Piotrowski, who turned up in Mexico in the 1840s. This was not a formalised migration. It probably resulted from efforts made by the Spanish authorities at the end of the 18th century to increase the output of the silver mines in the viceroyalties of Peru and New Spain, though one cannot rule out a connection between the Polish miners and the German-Mexican Mining Company (Compañía Minera Germano-Mexicana), founded in 1824, which was interested in exploiting Mexican silver deposits (Smolana 2018: 237).

Organized migration from Poland began only towards the end of the 19th century, but was never mass immigration. At the beginning of the 20th century, a small group of Poles came to Mexico; they included Prince Albert Stanisław Radziwiłł, who became a great landowner in the state of Nuevo León, and Dr Maysels, a wealthy factory owner active in the textile industry (Łepkowski 1970: 87). In the years 1870–1918, however, Polish-Mexican contacts weakened, and traces of Polishness in Mexico faded (Łepkowski 1970: 86), mainly because of the difficulties Poles in Mexico had in maintaining contact with their compatriots at home under the rule of the three occupying powers.

The interbellum period

A new stage in Polish-Mexican relations began when Poland regained its independence in 1918. Bilateral relations between the two states were properly established, but were not among the best as a result of the political reality of the time. Many differences existed between the principles that guided the pro-revolutionary Mexican authorities and those of the Polish authorities, especially after the May Coup in Poland. At the same time, in the policy of Poland, Mexico, unlike the Dominican Republic or Colombia, was not seen as a suitable place for organised Polish colonisation, with the result that Poland paid little attention to it. Nevertheless, during the interbellum period, the number of Polish immigrants in Mexico gradually rose.

Polish emigrants went to Mexico in considerable numbers, but were deprived for a long time of diplomatic care, since Poland's representation in Mexico City began only in 1929. In 1924, when the USA introduced immigration restrictions, the wave of migration from Poland diminished. Initially, most immigrants treated Mexico as a transit state on the long road leading mainly to the USA. By the end of the 1920s, that tendency had changed, with Mexico becoming a destination country. During the interbellum period, about 600 Poles a year moved to Mexico, many of whom were of Jewish origin, or Silesians belonging to the Salesians of Don Bosco order (Łepkowski 1970: 88).

It is estimated that, in 1932, 2,142 Poles were present in Mexico, of whom about 2,000 were of Jewish origin (Jacorzynski, Kozlowski 2015: 25). They settled mainly in urban centres and quickly became naturalised – in 1935, fewer than 1,200 of them still held Polish citizenship (Łepkowski 1970: 88). The ethnic composition of Mexican Polonia meant that its relationship with Poland and Mexico largely depended on the attitude of the authorities and societies in both states towards Jews. Polish Jews who came to Mexico in the 1920s did not maintain very close relations with the diplomatic representation of Poland, nor did they integrate very much with members of other Polish circles, though they did play a large role in developing trade relations between Poland and Mexico (Łepkowski 1980: 170–171). It was at their initiative that, in 1934, one of the most important companies for intensifying trade contacts with Poland during the interbellum period was established, namely, Compañía Mercantil Transmarítima, while in 1935 the Gulf Gdynia Line began sailing from Poland to Tampico. The largest turnover was seen in 1934, when Polish exports to Mexico were worth 1.5 million zlotys, and imports almost 1.1 million. Exports consisted mainly of plywood, paraffin, cigarette paper, gloves, kitchen utensils and brewer's barley. Imports from Mexico included coffee, sisal agave fibres, zinc blende, etc. (Łepkowski 1970: 89).

The end of the 1920s brought a slowdown in Polish migration to Mexico. This was due to both a tightening of migration policy in the USA, which was the target country for many Poles residing in Mexico, and to the Great Depression. The Mexican government attempted to protect itself against the crisis by first restricting, and ultimately stopping immigration. Slogans calling for the introduction of a restrictive immigration policy had begun to appear in Mexico earlier, especially in respect of three nationalities – Turks, Syrians and Poles, who often worked as private traders, competing against Mexican trading companies (Olejniczak 2007: 104). Despite the new immigration rules, further waves of migrants from Poland did reach Mexico, taking advantage of the weaknesses of the Mexican system – including a loophole that allowed families to be reconnected – and corruption among officials. Through France and Holland, more Poles made it to Mexico, such that their number went up from 3,000 to 3,500 (Olejniczak 2007: 105), where the majority continued to be people of Jewish origin. In 1931, in the context of the economic crisis, the 2nd Migration Congress banned economic immigration and permitted the deportation of foreigners who took on work other than what they had declared at the moment they entered Mexican territory. At the same time, the rule extended to all immigrants, including Poles, who were engaged in subversive activities among Mexican workers; this transferred into a significant decline in Polish immigration to Mexico.

It is hard to determine just how many Poles settled in Mexico, starting from the first waves of migration in the 19th century. Statistics show that in the first years after Poland regained its independence (1918–1924), the total number of people who travelled to Mexico and Cuba was 7,843 persons. In the following period, 1929–1931, that figure was 871. It is estimated that in the years 1918–1924, about 2,300 Poles went to Mexico, from 1925 to 1930 another 1,667, and from 1931 to 1937 it was 870. In total, in the 1920s, 3,609 people emigrated from Poland to Mexico, and in the following decade another 1,298 (Łepkowski 1980: 144), of which some went under the principle of reconnecting families. Some researchers say that during the interbellum period, the number of Polish immigrants in Mexico may even have reached 7,500 (Paradowska 1985: 123–124), of whom most were of Jewish origin and were engaged mainly in small trade and as craftsmen. The largest gatherings of Poles in Mexico were in Mexico City, Veracruz, Monterrey and Puebla.

As mentioned above, Mexican Polonia was long deprived of care from the Polish authorities. Nor was there any single centre coordinating the Poles scattered about the country. Members of the Polish diaspora made their own attempts to integrate Polonia. In Merida in the 1920s, at the initiative of the chemist Antoni Beździk, the first Polish association was formed – at first, it was called the Social and Cultural Union of Citizens of the Republic of Poland, later the Polonia Society. Despite a lack of support from the Polish authorities, the organisation functioned on its own, and by the end of the 1930 had about 3,000 members. In the first years of its existence, it acted quickly to help Polish citizens in Mexico, regardless of their faith or ethnic origins, take their first steps in their new environment, thereby taking a lot of the burden off the representation of France, which was responsible at that time for issuing documents to and taking care of Polish migrants. Yet, as a result of disputes it had with the Consul General of Poland, the Polonia Society had to temporarily disband its activities, and after being reactivated it never against achieved such a level of activity. Also at the initiative of Antoni Beździk, a Polish school was founded in Merida (Łepkowski 1980: 139). Polish Jews, in turn, mainly gathered in a club called "Tiferes Isroel". They also had a special school committee (Schulkomitet far Poijln). As Tadeusz Łepkowski writes, "in the opinion of the representation of the Republic of Poland, all those organisations were moderate in their relations with Poland, only once making a sharp declaration directed against incidents of anti-Jewish sentiment in Poland" (Łepkowski 1980: 164). The organizational efforts of Mexican Polonia, though laudable, were inadequate. Poles in Mexico could not count on help or support from the state of their motherland, and assimilated quite quickly – especially those of Jewish origin; they applied for Mexican citizenship in view of the passivity of the Polish authorities.

Only during World War II did the Polonia community in Mexico begin to strive for greater integration. In May 1940, the "Polish Union in Mexico – Unión Polonesa en México" – was established. Its programme assumptions included: to strive for solidarity among all those from Poland, to protect the interests of Poles in Mexico, and "reliable ideological and material work aimed at, to the extent possible, rebuilding a Poland that is strong, truly democratic and just, in which every citizen, regardless of origin or faith, will have equal obligations and be able to enjoy fully equal rights" (Smolana 2018: 293–294). The activities of the organisation, however, weakened considerably in the years that followed due to internal conflicts, and eventually led to a split from which emerged, among other bodies, the Polish Federation of Mexico.

In this period, Polish emigration was mainly from rural areas, and for economic reasons. A lack of land and hunger caused thousands of persons to emigrate to the New World in order to better themselves economically, especially that in many states of the Americas specially created colonisation companies purchased land and attracted Polish settlers. As part of the plan to create a "New Poland" in the western hemisphere, a plan was formed for bringing Polish colonists to the Mexican States of Sinaloa and Sonora, this was promoted intensively by the private colonisation company Sinaloa Company International SA, with the approval of the Mexican Ministry of Foreign Affairs (Olejniczak 2007: 109). In 1940, a similar initiative concerning Poles settling in the State of Chihuahua was announced by Polish MP Daniel Jensen, but this failed due to a lack of interest on the part of potential settlers. The main restrictions in this regard resulted from the provisions of the Mexican Constitution of 1917, which treated land as the property of the nation and prevented it from being disposed of freely. Migration to rural areas, then, was only symbolic, and during this period, no more than several dozen Polish peasants settled in Mexico. The process was also hindered by Mexican provisions of law, which gave preference to settlement by colonists re-emigrating from the USA.

The "Santa Rosa" refugees

During the World War II, a new wave of Polish emigrants came to Mexico, which can be divided into four groups. The first comprised intellectuals of Jewish origin who sailed to Mexico with passports issued by various countries. The second comprised scientists, journalists and artists, such as the geologist Feliks Sobota, the journalist Feliks T. Urbański, the musicians Maryla Lonas and Henryk Szeryng, and the writer Teodor Parnicki. The third group consisted of people connected with the Polish government-in-exile and employees of the Republic of Poland's representation in Mexico. The fourth group comprised about 1,500 Polish refugees, mainly women and children who, from 1943 to 1946, were resettled at a hacienda in Santa Rosa in León, in the State of Guanajuato (Łepkowski 1980: 298–302).

After the USSR invaded Poland on 17 September 1939, the Russians began deporting people from the territories they occupied; these included members of religious, national or ethnic minorities and well-to-do peasants, who were sent to Siberia and their property confiscated. It is estimated that at that time, from 500,000 to 2.5 million people were transported from Polish lands to the Soviet Union. Their situation changed when Germany attacked the USSR. On 30 July 1941, the Polish Prime Minister and Commander-in-Chief, Władysław Sikorski, signed an arrangement with the Soviet ambassador in London, Ivan Maisky, that restored diplomatic relations between Moscow and Poland. The agreement foresaw an amnesty for Poles imprisoned within the USSR and their forming an army which, along with the Red Army, was to fight the Germans on the eastern front. The Polish authorities-in-exile, in an understanding with Great Britain, began negotiations with the Soviet Union on evacuating the displaced persons to the Middle East and areas under British control. Beginning in 1942, the operation of evacuating and transporting Poles from the USSR to Iran began. The growing group of refugees in the Middle East – a total of about 100,000 Poles were evacuated from Russia – made it necessary to find an outlet for the migration pressure and to look for new areas where those people could settle. Initially, a request was made for the USA to accept the Polish refugees, but when Washington refused, consideration was also given to relocating them in Mexico – which agreed to accept 40,000. The relevant negotiations were conducted by General Sikorski, the head of the Polish government-in-exile; in 1942, he visited Mexico at the invitation of President Manuel Ávila Camacho (1940–1946).

In this way, Mexico became the only country in the world other than the British Commonwealth, and the only country in the western hemisphere, to help the Polish government resolve the humanitarian crisis that, in the winter of 1943, threatened thousands of Polish civilians living in temporary refugee camps in Persia and India. Ultimately, 1,500 people went to Mexico in the summer of 1943. Though there was a railway strike on at the time, Mexican workers decided to allow the train carrying the refugees to cross the border and take them to their destination without any stops. Poles from the Middle East, mainly women and children, were granted war refugee status – meaning they had the right to remain in Mexican territory until the end of the war, without the possibility of working or settling beyond the territory of their refugee camp.

The camp was organized at a hacienda in Santa Rosa in León, in the State of Guanajuato. It was financed out of funds from a special loan that the US President Franklin Delano Roosevelt offered General Sikorski. The interest-free credit was in the amount of 3 million USD, to be repaid after the end of the war. The Polish-Mexican agreement contained a proviso that if the number of Polish refugees increased, Mexico would not incur the cost of their upkeep. In exchange, the refugee camp was granted considerable internal autonomy. After the hacienda was renovated, it contained a medical clinic, dining room, children's playground and apartments for families. For the group of more than 200 Polish orphans, an orphanage was created in which education was provided by seven Polish Felician sisters who came from the USA for that purpose; in August 1943, the first lessons began in the Polish elementary and middle school situated within the camp. Usually in connection with state holidays, ceremonial gatherings, theatre plays and musical performances in regional costume, both within the camp and beyond, were systematically organised. In accordance with the Polish-Mexican agreement, the residents of Santa Rosa could not compete economically with the local population, and this posed quite a burden on the camp community. Over time, local cobbler's, tailor's and carpenter's workshops arose that provided camp residents with services for a small fee.

The Poles were welcomed very warmly in Mexico, which, given the wartime trauma they had suffered, was extremely important. One Santa Rosa resident, Anna Żarnecka de Burgoa, described the situation as follows: "It was incredible. After two years of hardship in Soviet camps, and then in camps in Iran and Calcutta, for the first time in three years we felt like people. Up till then we had been unwelcome intruders bringing along illness and suffering. Here we were welcomed like long-expected guests, and really, the feelings of gratitude and surprise we felt then were indescribable" (Piwowarczyk 2012).

The camp in Santa Rosa functioned for almost three years. On 9 July 1945, Mexico withdrew its recognition of the Polish government-in-exile and recognised the communist Provisional Government of National Unity. Consequently, a decision was taken to conclude the activities of the refugee camp; it ceased operating on 31 December 1946. A total 59 people returned to Poland, about 400 decided to remain in Mexico, while the rest managed to emigrate to the USA or Canada. Although this was a short episode, the camp in Santa Rosa had a positive impact on strengthening Polish-Mexican relations, forging bonds of solidarity between the two states (Smolana 2018: 334). It also inspired many artists, who are gradually uncovering the history of Polish refugees in Mexico. The story of the Santa Rosa camp became the subject of a documentary film by Sławomir Grünberg, "Santa Rosa: Odyssey in the Rhythm of Mariachi", and of another film titled "From Poland to Santa Rosa, after One Thousand Days", directed by Alejandro Hurtado de León and Berenice Sánchez Luna.

Issues of Polonia after 1945

After the end of the World War II, the political conditions did not favour a rapprochement between Poland and Mexico or the maintenance of relations between members of Polonia in Mexico and their country of origin. As a result, the Polish diaspora in Mexico began to slowly decompose. Many Poles, unenthusiastic about communism in Poland, no longer wanted to maintain relations with Polonia or the diplomatic representation of the Polish People's Republic, and this largely ended any chance of creating a cohesive Polonia.

In the first decades of the Cold War, especially under the right-wing governments of Miguel Alemán Valdés (1946–1952) and Adolfo Ruiz Cortines (1952–1958), Poles in Mexico were deprived of diplomatic care from the Polish People's Republic. The strong anti-communism of those governments, including the regime's establishment of a political police force – the National Security Directorate – meant that fears of possible repressions weakened the ties between Poles living in Mexico and their country of origin. Without contact with Poland, Poles in Mexico quickly assimilated, which slowed down the development of Polonia. Only along with the development of trade contacts in the late 1960s and early 1970s did the two states also take an interest in the situation of migrants, though in the case of the PPR authorities this was limited mainly to formal support for a small number of cultural initiatives within Polonia circles.

In 1982, a Committee for Support of Solidarity (El Comité de Apoyo a Soliadaridad) was established in Mexico. It had information on the situation in Poland translated into Spanish and distributed among Polonia circles in Latin

America, organised meetings of leaders of Solidarity gathered in the International Solidarity Office in Brussels, and meetings with union leaders. Poles in Mexico also initiated a campaign to send to Poland packages of coffee – a prized commodity at that time on the Polish black market. The proceeds from sales helped finance the activities of the Solidarity movement, financially support the families of dissidents, and pay lawyers for political prisoners (Jacorzyński, Kozłowski 2015: 30–31).

During the Cold War, the number of Poles in Mexico grew slowly but steadily, mainly with regard to mixed families; though, because of people's complex identities and the advanced process of assimilation, it is hard to say precisely how large that growth was. For example, according to the Mexican census of 1950, there were 3,464 people born in Poland living in Mexico, but only 1,379 of them declared Polish as their mother tongue. According to estimates calculated on the basis of censuses, the number of Poles in Mexico was as follows: 1,871 in 1960, 2,589 in 1970 and 3,031 in 1975 (Dobosiewicz, Rómmel 1977: 98). In the 1970s, however, the population of Mexican Polonia declined, due to many of its members emigrating to the USA, and to deepening assimilation.

Among the well-known Poles living in Mexico after World War II were the economist Miguel Wionczek, an advisor to President Luis Echevarría (1970–1976), the violinist Henryk Szeryng, the writer Teodor Parnicki, the poet and translator Jan Zych, the botanist Czesława Prywer Lidzbarska, and the physicist Jerzy Plebański, who in 1976 was awarded the Order of the Aztec Eagle (Orden de la Águila Azteca), the highest honour given to a foreigner for service to the Mexican nation. The best-known people of Polish origin in Mexico also include Elena Poniatowska, a Mexican writer who traces her roots back to the family of the last king of Poland, Stanisław August Poniatowski. The journalist Ryszard Kapuściński also spent several years in Mexico.

Mexico and Poland were brought closer together by Karol Wojtyła, that is, Pope John Paul II. He visited Mexico five times, calling it his "second homeland" (segunda patria). He also played an instrumental part in the beatification in 1990 and canonisation in 2003 of Juan Diego, an aboriginal Mexican. His visits to Mexico also served to mobilise the Polish community, though for a short time, to become more integrated.

In general, though, the Polish community in Mexico is younger than in other Latin American countries, having formed only during the interbellum period and being quite well assimilated in the Mexican society. Mexicans of Polish origin tend to be well educated – they are usually scientists, artists or musicians. In the second half of the 20th century, Poland settled in Mexico only sporadically, most often as a result of mixed marriages or contracts. As Dorota K. Olejniczak writes, however, "unfortunately, this group long went unnoticed by the Polish author-ities. This is shown by the fact that there was no Polish representation there for quite a long time, while formal care of Polish citizens was exercised by the French consul" (Olejniczak 2007: 100). That situation changed only after 1989, when the first attempts were made to reorganise Mexican Polonia; two honorary consuls of the Republic of Poland were appointed, in Monterrey and Guadalajara, and the Polish Order of Pallottine monks began functioning in Mexico.

It is difficult to determine the current number of Poles living in Mexico. According to a census of the year 2000, 1,943 people declared themselves to be of Polish nationality, but we should bear in mind the very advanced process of assimilation among Poles in Mexico. Estimates most often speak of a group of from 1,500 to 2,500 people, including about 1,000 in Mexico City itself[21]. Most live in the federal district, Xalapa, Guadalajara, Puebla, Cuernavaca, Guanajuato and Monterrey. In addition, in Mexico there are about 15,000 descendants of Jews who came from various parts of Poland (Jacorzyński, Kozłowski 2015: 32)[22].

State policy towards Polonia

The legal basis for cooperation between Poland and Polonia is the Constitution of the Republic of Poland of 2 April 1997, where Article 6 par. 2 stipulates: "The Republic of Poland shall provide assistance to Poles living abroad to maintain their links with the national cultural heritage" and Article 36 states: "A Polish cit-izen shall, during a stay abroad, have the right to protection by the Polish State".

In addition, the Act of 4 September 1997 on Departments of Government Administration (Art. 32, par. 2 pt. 1) states that the minister of foreign affairs is obliged to develop and submit for consideration by the Council of Ministers a long-term foreign policy strategy, while Regulation No. 70 of the President of the Council of Ministers of 27 June 2008 on the Creation of an Inter-ministerial Team for Matters concerning Polonia and Poles Abroad stipulates that the duties of the minister of foreign affairs include "developing and monitoring the

---

21 Other estimates speak of about 3,000 first-generation Poles in Mexico, or even 15,000 descendents of Polish immigrants, mainly of Jewish descent. Komisja pozytywnie o kandydatach na ambasadorów w Meksyku i Kostaryce oraz na Słowacji, "Gazeta Prawna", 06.06.2018, www.gazetaprawna.pl. (accessed: 30.07.2018).

22 At the same time, according to the National Population and Housing Census of 2011, there are 523 Mexican nationals living in Poland. Narodowy Spis Ludności i Mieszkań 2011, Główny Urząd Statystyczny (GUS), Warszawa 2015, p.135.

implementation by government administration of the government programme on cooperation with Polonia and Poles abroad".

The "Government programme on cooperation with Polonia and Poles abroad in the years 2015–2020" approved by the Council of Ministers is intended as an answer to that challenge: to enable migrants to maintain ties with Poland, to create an attractive offer of cooperation for the young generation of Polonia, to make better use of the potential of Polish professionals abroad, and to effectively secure the rights of Polish minorities on the principle of a cooperative partnership with Polonia.

Within that programme, the Ministry of Foreign Affairs proposes that its Polonia partners make joint, bilateral use of campaigns promoting Poland's good image abroad and deepening cooperation between Poland and the countries they live in, both regionally (e.g. through local governments) and sectorally (e.g. through universities, cultural institutions and business entities). New in the current programme are a specification of the rules of the government's cooperation with Polonia and Poles abroad, and an emphasis on partnership. The strategic goals of the programme are: to support teaching of the Polish language, teaching in Polish and teaching about Poland; to strengthen Polish identity and ensure the possibility of taking part in national culture; to strengthen Polish communities abroad; to support the return of Poles to Poland and create incentives for people of Polish descent to settle in Poland; and to develop contacts with Poland on many levels.

Poland's policy towards Polonia and Poles abroad is part of its foreign policy. By a decision of parliament, funds from the state budget allocated for that purpose were approved in 2012 by the Ministry of Foreign Affairs. In this way, the government, and in practice the Ministry of Foreign Affairs, obtained an instrument in the form of a targeted reserve increasing the possibility of effectively implementing state tasks within the scope of cooperation with Polonia and Poles abroad. The particular aspects of the programme are dealt with by the department of the Ministry of Foreign Affairs responsible for policy towards Polonia and Poles abroad, by territorial departments (in the case of Mexican Polonia – the Department of the Americas), and also by the consular department and in public diplomacy for promoting Poland.

"Polish Foreign Policy Priorities 2012–2016", approved by the Council of Ministers in March 2012, sets out the most important direction and tasks for the government's foreign policy. In cooperation with Polonia and Poles abroad, the Polish government is guided by the principles of: partnership; Polish culture as the common good of all Poles, regardless of where they live; appreciation of the role Poles abroad play in forming friendly relations between Poland and the countries where they live; and appreciation of their material and cultural contributions to the development of those countries. At the same time, the Polish government, recognising that a large majority of Polonia and Poles abroad are citizens of other countries and are loyal to those countries, considers that the most effective level for bilateral cooperation is acting to maintain Poland's good image around the world and to develop multilateral cooperation with a given country or region where Poles live.

Thus, the strategic policy goals towards Polonia and Poles abroad focus on: supporting teaching of the Polish language, teaching in Polish, and teaching about Poland among Polonia and Poles living abroad and to the children of migrant workers; maintaining and strengthening Polish identity; ensuring opportunities to take part in national culture; strengthening the position of Polonia circles through enhancing the effectiveness of their activities; increasing their activities in public life in the countries of residence and popularising knowledge of the rights they enjoy; supporting the return of Poles to Poland; and developing youth, scientific, cultural, economic, sports and local government contacts with Poland. Of key importance are: developing ties of the young generation with Poland by promoting direct contacts and travel to Poland; tying the economic potential of Polonia and Poles abroad to the economic development of Poland; and supporting Polonia business endeavours, new forms of communication with Poland and public opinion in the country.

The programme distinguishes ten geographic and functional groups among Polonia and Poles abroad. Among those are a mere two Latin American states – Brazil and Argentina – in ninth place. So we can conclude that Mexican Polonia finds itself in the last category – "other states". This group includes countries in which a small number of Poles reside who function under widely varying conditions and have different origins. In this category, cooperation and access to national culture and Polish language teaching is limited organisationally by the dispersal of the Polonia communities. Government actions should concentrate on supporting cultural initiatives, creating conditions for Polish language teaching and integrating Polonia communities (Government cooperation programme 2015: 14).

The strategy distinguishes four groups of Poles abroad. The most important criteria for dividing them is the type of bonds that connect a group with Poland, their level of knowledge of Polish, their potential to mobilise others within the country of residence, their level of self-identification with Poland, their cultural heritage and current interests and, as a result, their type and level of engagement in cooperation with Poland. For the needs of the programme, a distinction was also made between a) Polish minorities; b) Polonia; c) emigration from the period of World War II and the following decades; and d) migration after Poland's EU accession in 2004 through the free movement of people within the European Union. Under this typology, Poles in Mexico are counted in the second and third categories. Polonia, then, should be understood as the collective of people born outside Poland whose ancestors left Poland. People who belong to Polonia maintain their ties with national traditions and culture into the second generation, and usually beyond. They treat their connections with Poland as part of their family history – and thus of their own history. Often, members of Polonia communities have never been to Poland or have visited it only sporadically. Their knowledge of the Polish language has either disappeared or (usually) is limited; this factor must be taken into account when choosing the language of communication with Polonia. Their level of identification with Polish issues varies – from distanced to affirmative. In many countries, Polonia is well established and has significant, though untapped potential to mobilise people. Its involvement in cooperation with Poland concerns strictly defined areas, for example, promoting culture, business, investments and the historical legacy. To a lesser degree, among the Poles in Mexico there are those who emigrated in the period during and after the World War II, for a variety of reasons (political, economic, ethnic), and who are usually strongly connected with Poland by ties of family and citizenship, their mother tongue, and patriotism.

At present in Mexico, several Polonia organisations are active, such as the Union of Poles and Friends of Poland in Mexico, the Association of Poles in Mexico (Asociación Polaco Mexicana), and the Mexican Delegacy of the World Federation of Polish Veterans' Associations. At the Polish embassy in Mexico, there is also a School Consultation Point that runs courses on the Polish language, and in Polish, for children. And there are spontaneous, individual gatherings of Poles in Mexico, and of cooperation to promote Polish culture and maintain ties with Poland. One example is AmaPola, a project that aims to promote Polish culture in Mexico and unite Poles living there[23].

Cooperative activities with Mexican Polonia are a part of the overall Latin American policy of the Republic of Poland – which does not make full use of its potential, and has not created an effective lobby for promoting positive bilateral relations. The biggest challenges facing Polish foreign policy in the context of improving contacts with Poles in Mexico are the fact that they are so widely spread out, and that many of them are largely assimilated. It is even difficult to

---

23 Dla Polaków, http://amapolamexico.blogspot.com/p/dla-polakow.html (accessed: 08.07.2018).

estimate the current size of Mexican Polonia, and so figures differ considerably. This is just one reason why Mexico did not even appear in the "Atlas of Polish Presence in the World" – an attempt to estimate the global scale of Polish emigration published by the Ministry of Foreign Affairs. It should also be borne in mind that the priority of Polonia policy is still directed eastward; the western hemisphere, with a small number of exceptions such as the USA, Canada, Argentina and Brazil, is not treated as seriously.

Apart from lofty declarations, there is little evidence of the will of both sides to engage and deepen direct contacts. Polonia in Mexico seems to be largely left to itself, which, given the rate of assimilation in Mexican society and its members' diminishing knowledge of the Polish language, could have catastrophic and irreversible consequences. Despite these objective difficulties, at key moments Poles in Mexico are able to mobilise themselves politically, take part in elections and make their voices heard on important matters concerning Poland's internal and international policy, though on such issues as well, Polonia circles are divided[24]. In 2017, during the first-ever visit by a Polish president to Mexico, Andrzej Duda met with Mexican Polonia, and emphasised the significance of its most active members in building bilateral relations. He awarded the singer Leszek Zawadka with the Knight's Cross of the Order of Polonia Restituta "for distinguished service to Polish culture, for achievements in artistic and creative work, and for activities for the benefit of the Polish community in Mexico". President Duda also awarded the Knight's Cross of the Order of Service to the Republic of Poland, "for distinguished service in popularising Polish culture and history, and for activities on behalf of the Polish community in Mexico" to: Marek Adamski, Luis Decelis Maciak, Hanna Kot-Arredondo, Józef Olechowski, Andrzej Rattinger-Aranda and dr Wiesław Skowroński. He expressed his thanks to Polonia that it belongs to the elite of Mexican society: "You are that Polonia, Poles of whom the Republic can certainly be not only proud, but towards whom it should be deeply grateful for your building the best possible image of Poland in the world," and emphasised that, in addition to engagement in the field of culture, economic ties should be developed as well[25]. The policy on Polonia promoted by the government of Poland in recent years is aimed at leading to an effective use of the

24 In 2017, Mexican Polonia organised protests after the Polish government recalled the Polish honorary consul, Alberto Stebelski-Orłowski, after he declined to accept the Order of Merit of the Republic of Poland from the hands of President Andrzej Duda as a sign of protest against developments in the internal situation in Poland.
25 First, a meeting with Polonia. Andrzej Duda awards members of Polonia in Mexico for service. "W Polityce", 24 kwietnia 2017, https://wpolityce.pl/

potential of Polonia worldwide, including in Mexico. Perhaps that policy will provide an impulse for greater activity on the part of Polish circles in Mexico, and for their greater involvement in maintaining contacts with Poland and developing bilateral relations.

***

Seen against the background of Polish communities in South America, Mexican Polonia has a number of specific characteristics. First of all, it is a small group, relatively young, concentrated mainly in urban centres. Historically, Mexico has never been considered as a place of Polish settlement, more as a transit country for Polish migrants on their way to the USA or other countries in the western hemisphere. More numerous emigration from areas of Poland, mainly for economic reasons, began only towards the end of the 19th century, and peaked during the period between the two world wars. Interestingly, most such immigrants to Mexico were of Jewish descent, and assimilated into Mexican society quite quickly. Deprived at first of care from the Polish state, they integrated on their own and willingly engaged in initiatives aimed at bringing Poland and Mexico close to each other. A glorious chapter in the history of the two countries' bilateral relations was during the World War II, when Mexico agreed to take in Polish refugees, some of whom at the end of the war decided to remain in Mexico. During the Cold War, there were very few cases of people migrating from Poland to Mexico, due to ideological differences between the two states and the obstacles to travelling out of Poland. Since 1989, the scale of migration has remained at a low level.

Poles in Mexico are widely dispersed throughout the country, mainly in large cities, which has considerably hindered the development of a strong Polonia. This lack of strong interest in activating Mexican Polonia also led to its becoming institutionalised to only a small degree. Yet, Poles in Mexico strive to maintain contacts with Poland, keep track of events there and involve themselves, to the extent they are able, in the political and artistic life of the country.

In recent years, Poland has been making efforts to step up its activities with regard to Polonia circles around the world. It seems, though, that the potential of Mexican Polonia is not fully appreciated or taken advantage of by Polish decision-makers. Mexican Polonia's modest significance is evident in the fact that it is not among the priority direction of Polish policy within this scope,

---

spoleczenstwo/336834-na-poczatek-spotkanie-z-polonia-andrzej-duda-odznaczyl-zasluzonych-w-dzialalnosci-polonijnej-w-meksyku-zobacz-zdjecia (accessed: 10.07.2018).

and is not even listed among important American and Latin American states. Though they are not a large group, Poles in Mexico often occupy important positions in Mexican society, especially in professions broadly connected with the arts and culture. It would seem appropriate, then, not only to maintain contact with them and support their efforts to integrate, but also to encourage them to create an energetic, effective lobby to promote enhanced cooperation between Poland and Mexico. For it is Mexican Polonia that is best informed about the mood of Mexican society, and its problems and preferences in terms of economic contacts, or the specifics of the local market. Considering the high degree of assimilation and the low level of knowledge of the Polish language among Poles in Mexico, it would be worth focusing on providing access to the mother tongue, increasing opportunities for learning it, running student exchanges and increasing the involvement of Mexican Polonia in building up a positive image of Poland, not only in the context of historical policy, but also as a state that is modern, developed and open.

With the rapid rate of assimilation among the Polish community in Mexico, marginalizing those people could lead to an irreversible loss of the ability to activate them, and to their becoming discouraged from maintaining further contacts with Poland – that is, to an enormous waste of their potential. On the other hand, a prudent, long-term policy of encouraging Poles in Mexico to become more involved in Polonia matters, taking account of all of the limitations of the community related to their dispersion and small numbers, but also taking account of their expectations and opportunities, and supporting efforts at integration, can result in the creation of a solid foundation for real understanding between the two states, and of the strategic partnership announced by President Andrzej Duda during his visit to Mexico in 2017.

Conclusion

"Poland and Mexico share similar values and take similar positions on many issues, such as the need to strengthen democracy and the rule of law, the protection of human rights, energy security and free trade" (Polish-Mexican political consultations). Vice Minister of Foreign Affairs Szymon Szynkowski vel Sęk emphasised the above levels of cooperation as the most important for mutual understanding between states, during the 11th round of Polish-Mexican political consultations held in Warsaw on 14 June 2018.

Mexico was one of the only three Latin American countries directly mentioned in "The Information of the Minister of Foreign Affairs on the tasks of Polish foreign policy in 2019" which underlined the objectives of Polish foreign policy towards Latin American states: "in relations with Latin America the main challenge of the last three years was to create favourable conditions for the comprehensive development of cooperation, especially in the economic sphere. The basis for optimism is the stable economic and social situation in the leading countries of the continent, the progressive liberalisation of trade with the European Union and the strong and established presence of the Polish community in the region (…). We strive to develop relations with Mexico on the basis of a presidential declaration signed in April 2017. Nn the capital of Mexico we have opened the first PAIH in the region. We have also ensured a Polish presence in the PA (Mexico, Colombia, Peru and Chile), currently the most dynamically developing bloc in the region, aiming to strengthen our cooperation in the field of trade and investment" (Informacja Ministra Spraw Zagranicznych o zadaniach polskiej polityki zagranicznej w 2019 roku).

It would seem, then, that bilateral relations are based on a solid foundation and are moving towards the implementation of the strategic partnership announced a year earlier by Presidents Andrzej Duda and Enrique Peña Nieto. After many years of being on the fringes of Poland's foreign policy with Latin American states, increasing attention is now being drawn to the potential of and opportunities for effective cooperation with Mexico. One can also observe an appreciation of the position of Mexico, which is emerging in one of Poland's most important political and economic partners in Latin America. While it is true that Mexico had previously been mentioned in the official rhetoric as a priority direction for Poland's engagement in the region, in reality the attention of Polish decision-makers was concentrated primarily on South American countries such as Argentina, Brazil and Chile, which, in addition to the economic opportunities they offered, are also home to large numbers of Polish émigrés.

At the beginning of the 21st century, Mexico was ranked among those countries having significant potential to form global relations, and even as an emerging power. Its good economic results and ambitious internal reforms took place along with a change in its international self-narration and an activation of its engagement around the world. On the wave of alliances established by developing countries, in 2011, Goldman Sachs counted Mexico among the MIKT group of significant emerging economies (Mexico, Indonesia, South Korea and Turkey); after Australia joined, the group became known as MIKTA. Another attempt to place Mexico among those countries with great potential for development was an initiative by Jim O'Neill, who in 2014 proposed the name MINT (Mexico, Indonesia, Nigeria and Turkey) for those countries, which in the near future will shape the world economy (Oberda Monkiewicz 2016: 558). Thus, Mexico has become an important element of the new emerging economies towards which the attention of the main global players is being turned.

Poland has also gradually begun to appreciate Mexico's growing importance, not only regionally, but globally; it was this that led to the declaration on establishing a strategic partnership in bilateral relations, since "the intention of building strategic relations is based on clear growth in recent years in the level of relations between the two countries, on regular political contacts at a high level, on shared democratic values, and on mutual support for the aspirations of the other side in international forums" (Joint Communiqué of the Mexican and Polish Ministries of Foreign Affairs 2018: 1). The partnership announced in 2017 reflects the growing position of Mexico in Poland's foreign policy and the two states' reciprocal will to deepen existing relations. Up to now, their bilateral relations have been proper and without serious controversies, but have not been very dynamic, and Mexico, unlike other Latin American countries, remained on the periphery of Poland's international agenda.

Mexico's encouraging economic results, relatively stable internal situation and increasingly active presence in multilateral organisations have all caused it to be seen as an important partner in the context of diversifying Poland's economic relations and political alliances. Without doubt, Polish-Mexican relations have been affected by Mexico's good relations with the European Union, with which Mexico is connected by both a strategic association and an Economic Partnership, Political Coordination and Cooperation Agreement (Global Agreement). Since the Global Agreement entered into force in 2000, trade exchange between the signatories has grown by about 8% annually, giving total trade growth of 148% (the EU and Mexico also concluded a new trade agreement in 2018), while a new understanding negotiated in 2018, which practically abolished customs duty in trade relations, may prove to be even more beneficial for the two parties concerned. Closer relations with Mexico are also favoured by the policy initiated by President Enrique Peña Nieto of intensifying relations with Europe, etc., and of seeking new markets in answer to the exhaustion of the formula of integration offered by NAFTA and the crisis in Mexico's relations with the administration of Donald Trump.

Poland is responding to Mexico's strategy, and is trying to take advantage of the favourable international situation by engaging in economic diplomacy as promoted by President Duda and seeking to diversify its economic partners. One can say, therefore, that the circumstances are indeed favourable for a strategic partnership, and that the foundations laid over many years are solid and stable.

What, then, connects Poland and Mexico? Despite the two countries' differences in language and culture, and the great distance between them, a number of similarities and stable tendencies in their bilateral relations can be identified. In fact, Poland was once called the "Mexico of Europe". Up to now, that phrase had mainly a negative association – it could refer to similarities in traditional religious structure (Catholicism dominates in both countries) or economics, since both were perceived mainly as sources of cheap labour. Today, such an expression is much more multifaceted. For, like Mexico, Poland is a country betting on stable economic growth, that can boast of better and better macroeconomic results, and whose role in international economic organisations is growing systematically. After years of cautious or passive and not fully autonomous foreign policy, both states are intensifying their presence on the international scene, both regionally and globally, as can be seen, for example, in their cooperation within the United Nations.

Though thousands of kilometres apart, Poland and Mexico also have similar historical experience involving hard struggles for independence, foreign interventionism, military occupation and painful losses of territory. They are also joined by their complicated geopolitical positions, which on more than one occasion have determined the scope of their international engagement. Mexico, which borders the USA, has remained under the influence of Washington, which has affected both the form of Mexico's internal policy and its international alliances. Poland, lying between two strong European powers – Germany and Russia – has also had to adjust its activities to the complex rivalry between those two, and has sometimes fallen victim to their expansion; during the Cold War, Poland found itself in the socialist camp dominated by the USSR, and its sovereignty was seriously limited.

The economies of the two countries also have a similar structure and face similar problems. In both cases, there is a chance for development in joining broad
processes of regional integration; for Mexico, this meant acceding to the North
American Free Trade Agreement in 1994, while for Poland it was achieving
membership in the European Union ten years later. NAFTA and the EU were
milestones for Mexico and Poland, and accession advanced their economic
development, though there were both benefits and drawbacks.

The foreign policy of each of the two states is largely conditioned by their
internal policies, which largely determine their international alliances and the
main directions for their global engagement. Both Poland and Mexico have travelled the long, hard road to democracy, and the process of consolidation continues. For both, the EU and United States are important allies, though recently
a certain evolution in how they are perceived has been observable. One example
of this is how perceptions of the USA have changed in Mexico during the term
of office of Donald Trump. Controversial statements by the American president
concerning the US's neighbour to the south led to a radicalisation of anti-A-
merican feeling in Mexico, and were an important factor in the loss suffered by
the PRI (Partido Revolucionario Institucional – the Institutional Revolutionary
Party) in the Mexican presidential election in 2018. In Poland, the right-wing
government found common ground with Trump, as seen by the reception he
received during his visit to Warsaw in 2017. At the same time, there has also
been an intensification of Mexico's contacts with the EU and a relative weakening
of Poland's relations with the EU, though these remain an important reference
point for both states.

Polish-Mexican bilateral relations are also distinguished by a kind of
unchangeability in diplomatic relations, for "representatives of Poland accredited
in Mexico usually extend their presence there more often than their counterparts
in Poland. Thus, the first tendency resulting from our diplomatic relations is the
contrast between the stability of Polish diplomatic and consular personnel in
Mexico and the high turnover of Mexican foreign affairs officials in Poland"
(Moloeznik 2007: 132). Further, one can observe an accumulation by Poland of
diplomatic posts; this results from limited finances, but also from the small role
Latin American countries have played in Poland's foreign policy. Representatives
of Poland accredited in Mexico have usually also acted as ambassadors in
neighbouring countries. Up to 2017, the Polish ambassador to Mexico was also
responsible for relations with Central American and Caribbean states. Today,
after the opening of the embassy in Panama, the ambassador in Mexico is also
accredited in Costa Rica. At the same time, diplomatic relations are friendly, and
do not generate contentious issues. It is also worth recalling that Mexico was

one of three Latin American states (along with Argentina and Brazil) in which Poland established diplomatic relations and permanent representation.

According to some researchers, another factor that in certain periods of time has been equally important in determining the dynamics of Polish-Mexican relations is the relation between the state and the Catholic Church – whether positive or negative. This was particularly evident in the interbellum period, when "the importance and historical influence of the Catholic Church in Poland contrasts with the anti-clerical attitude of the Mexican Revolution (1910–2917) and further post-revolutionary governments right up to 1988... This clash between the traditional approach of the Polish government towards the Catholic Church and the rejection of the spiritual hierarchy by Mexico affected the relations between the two countries" (Moloeznik 2007: 137). These divergences were especially evident during the "Cristeros" uprising in Mexico (1927–1929), and resulted in, for example, a delay in the appointment of a diplomatic representative of the Republic of Poland. Poland even considered intervening in the internal affairs of Mexico and supplying the Catholic insurgents with arms (Moloeznik 2007: 138). The changes introduced by President Carlos Salinas de Gortari in 1988, and the abolition of communism in Poland a year later, removed the existing barriers. Another factor that was of extremely positive importance to the rapprochement between the two countries was the active role played Pope John Paul II – Poland's best ambassador to Mexico. The Pope visited Mexico several times, mobilising Mexican Polonia to greater integration and maintaining Poland's positive image in Mexican society. Today as well, the Polish Ministry of Foreign Affairs emphasises that those factors that favour cooperation with the states of Latin America and the Caribbean, including Mexico, are: "a community of Christian and democratic values, allegiance to the rules of international law, and the need to enforce the law"[26].

In the geopolitical context, primary emphasis is placed on the nature of the two states as gateways (Moloeznik 2007: 144), where "a convergence of interests between Poland and Mexico is characteristic of the current and future relations of the two powers in the complicated and uncertain international scenario. Both countries can and must bring as much understanding as possible to the development of relations between Europe and Latin America. Latin America, of which

---

26 Ministry of Foreign Affairs, Relations of Poland with countries of Latin America and the Caribbean, https://www.msz.gov.pl/pl/polityka_zagraniczna/inne_kontynenty/ ameryka_lacinska_i_karaiby/stosunki_dwustronne_ameryka_lacinska_karaiby/ stosunki_polska___ameryka_lacinska_i_karaiby (accessed: 15.07.2018).

Mexico is a part, belongs to the West, and is an heir of European culture, of which Poland, in turn, is an important representative. At the beginning of the 21st century, both countries, Poland and Mexico, must accept much and change much, and this lies within the remit not only of the diplomatic and consular services, but also of the artistic, cultural and academic scenes, where the cultivation of bilateral relations has its weight and continuity". Aware of the limitations imposed by their geopolitical situations, both Poland and Mexico are striving not only to overcome these, but to make them an important attribute in their regional and global relations, acting as intermediaries in relations between their neighbouring states and facilitating access to regional centres.

What, then, has shaped bilateral relations in the past and is shaping them today? Despite certain unfavourable international and geographic circumstances, Polish-Mexican relations have a long history. They were initiated by Polish officers and soldiers, who entered Mexico at the beginning of the 19th century when it was fighting for independence, or were escaping from repressions after failed uprisings for Polish independence. Later, there were waves of economic migrants, for whom Mexico was only to be a transit country on the way to the USA or other countries in Latin American or the Caribbean, but often ended up becoming their second homeland.

Poland regained its independence in 1918 and, despite the difficult internal and international situations of each country, official diplomatic relations were established in 1928 and have continued without interruption to the present day. There are no contentious issues between Poland and Mexico; in fact, there is a noticeable reciprocal will to deepen the existing contacts between them. At the same time, despite the friendly rhetoric from both sides emphasising the increasing importance of bilateral relations, those relations in fact have only a marginal place in foreign policy. Political relations are proper, as seen in the high degree of convergence in the positions of Poland and Mexico in international organisations, and in the gradual intensification of their bilateral relations. Neither Poland nor Mexico is demanding changes in the international system, but they do seek to take advantage of the positive aspects of the process of globalisation to increase their bargaining position in international relations. In the realm of political relations, however, there does exist a need to intensify direct contacts at various levels, especially through regular consultations between their ministers of foreign affairs. Another important aspect worthy of being activated is parliamentary cooperation, not only at the level of their national parliaments, but also in regional and global organisations such as the Inter-Parliamentary Union or the EU-Mexico Joint Parliamentary Commission. Though political relations are in order, they are quite superficial, limited to courtesy visits, and only recently at a high level, and to irregular sectoral consultations; above all, they constitute a framework for economic cooperation, which the two countries both treat as a priority.

This intensification of economic relations, and especially of trade exchange, is taking place amid a certain destabilisation of the two countries' traditional directions that is forcing them to find new economic partners and new markets. This was the case, for example, after 2008 and the economic crisis that affected the member states of the European Union, but is also a consequence of a relative weakening of the economic ties under NAFTA that has resulted from the radical policy of the Donald Trump administration in Washington. These events affected both Poland and Mexico, pushing them to activate their foreign policies and search for new allies and economic partners. In the case of Poland, one factor that certainly created greater interest in Latin America was Poland's accession to the EU, which already had a long tradition of relations with the Latin America and the Caribbean region, a wide network of contacts there, and effective instruments for cooperating with non-European states[27].

Even though the structures of the two countries' economies are quite similar, and during the 1990s they actually competed over development funds, more and more frequently they see a chance for deepening cooperation in sectors such as energy, infrastructure and new technologies. They are aware of their structural limitations, but also aware of the need for continuous, sustainable development, which they treat as the key to increasing their ability to act in the international arena.

Traditionally, economic cooperation between Poland and Mexico has not been very intensive, with a trade exchange balance that is small, usually negative for Poland, and well below the opportunities for and potential of cooperation between them. At the same time, they have come up against a series of challenges that have hindered their forging closer economic relations. One could even speak of a kind of "historical determinism" that has meant that, despite the continual efforts and good will of the two states, economic relations have not intensified visibly (Moloeznik 2007: 136). As early as the 1920s, the Organizing

---

27 Yet one can also find opinions that Poland seems to be "a brake" on the process of deepening cooperation between the EU and Latin America and the Caribbean, because a condition for exploiting the potential of the two regions is reform of the EU Common Agricultural Policy, which the farming lobby in Poland is not keen on. Marcin F. Gawrycki, Polityka Polski wobec państw Ameryki Łacińskiej, [in]: Stanisław Bieleń (ed.), Polityka zagraniczna Polski po wstąpieniu do NATO i do Unii Europejskiej. Problemy tożsamości i adaptacji, Warsaw 2010, Difin, p. 429.

Committee of the Polish-Latin American Chamber of Commerce sent a trade mission to Mexico to pre-analyse the possibility of deepening trade exchange, but this brought no positive results. Further attempts to intensify economic relations ended similarly. Today as well, even though Poland holds a high position among its Latin American economic partners, its trade exchange with Mexico is not impressive, and remains well below the two countries' trade potential. The recent visit by President Duda to Mexico in 2017 was to provide an impulse for intensifying contacts within this scope; it was part of a broader strategy of economic diplomacy aimed at increasing trade exchange and searching for new markets for Polish products. At that time, the first outlet of the Foreign Trade Office of the Polish Investment and Trade Agency in Latin America and the Caribbean was established. The most important goal now is to implement the understandings signed and on that basis build effective, reciprocally beneficial cooperation.

Yet, increasing economic contacts will still require considerable effort. Poland does not have a well-established tradition of trade with Mexico, lacks knowledge of the specifics and expectations of the market there, and has no effective lobby acting to bring businesses from both states closer to each other, in either the public or private sector. An economic offer that is attractive to the other partner must be developed, to the extent possible and with the financial means available, as must a long-term strategy for building a stable position for Poland on the Mexican market and expanding economically. Other problems include certain mutual perceptions, a lack of awareness of the potential of the partner's market, existing protectionist barriers (both tariff and bureaucratic) and unregulated issues concerning veterinary regulations. Elements that can facilitate mutual understanding may include a similar style of doing business in which informal relations and direct contacts are most important, the absence of negative stereotypes resulting from shared history, and a growing command of English in both countries that makes it possible to overcome linguistic barriers.

Another factor that may serve to intensify economic relations is the position of each state as a bridge to its region – Mexico is connected economically with North America, but at the same time is a gateway to Central America and the Caribbean, and on to the Pacific; Poland is a member of the European Union, which includes the important market of Central and Eastern Europe. Much importance is also attached to the new Global Agreement between Mexico and the EU, seen as one of the most effective instruments of economic cooperation, and to Mexico's membership in the PA. The network of international and global institutional ties of the two states brings tremendous value to their bilateral relations.

Cultural relations, being less controversial, became a virtual substitute for normal political relations during the Cold War. Resistant to ideological differences, they are effective at binding relations between states, and constitute the best foundation for real understanding and the strategic partnership declared. It is worth considering, then, offering cultural events that not only concern historical and religious policy, but also bring to Mexican audiences the latest achievements in Polish art, literature and music. Given the limited means available for this, it makes sense to make an appropriate selection of these based on the interests and expectations of the local market.

One area of cooperation that has been developing increasingly intensively in recent years is that of relations in the field of education and science. Poland and Mexico have opened up to student exchanges, which are gradually expanding, and have intensified contacts among representatives of higher education. This is facilitating mutual exchanges among academics, and is leading to the initiation of joint projects that may result in innovations and long-term scientific cooperation. What is more, through more frequent direct contacts due to the growing number of Polish tourists, students and businesses in Mexico, mutual knowledge and social awareness will also grow, and this is the best way to eliminate the negative associations that impede mutual understanding. Mexico is perceived ambiguously in Poland. On the one hand, stereotypes abound that it is internally unstable, riddled with violence and a high crime rate. On the other hand, it is a state that respects traditional values, is associated with the Catholic faith and family, and has an exotic and attractive culture. Mexicans are perceived positively in Poland as people who enjoy life, and are resourceful and hardworking.

In the context of building up a positive image of Poland abroad and creating an effective pro-Polish lobby, another factor to consider is the Polish minority in Mexico. Unnoticed and unappreciated for many years because of its small size compared with Polonia in other countries in North and South America, it could not count on appropriate support from the Polish authorities, which meant that its members assimilated quickly and lost contact with their country of origin. Consequently, the small, widely dispersed groups of Poles in Mexico did not create a cohesive Polonia community and did not institutionalise their activities. Strengthening their efforts to integrate and meet their expectations that the state will become more active in promoting Polish language, culture and science will not only maintain the connections of Mexican Polonia with Poland, but will also make it possible to draw on its potential for intensifying bilateral relations.

Referring to the main thesis of the book, we are at the beginning of creating the foundations of a real partnership between states. Historically, it was not possible due to geographic distance or historical experience. At the time when

Mexico was built, the Polish state did not exist on the map divided between the partition states, and when Poland regained its independence, Mexico was in the middle of revolution that was shaping its present face. Direct contacts were rare and thus mutual knowledge as well. The political priorities of the two countries in the early days of their statehood were rather focused on the immediate environment. During the Cold War, both states remained on the various sides of the Iron Curtain, which also did not facilitate the agreement and did not foster the deepening of mutual relations. It was only the end of the 20th century that it had the opportunity to normalise relations between states. The internal transformations of both countries and their policy of diversification of external partners have contributed to deepening the mutual contacts. In the case of Poland, an important breakthrough in opening up to Latin American partners, including Mexico, was acquiring the membership in the European Union. The symbolic moment became when the Polish President, for the first time in bilateral history, paid visit to Mexico in 2017 and the Partnership Declaration was signed. This document foresees a stronger bilateral relationship, with particular emphasis on economic cooperation. It reflected largely the interest of both countries, established a formal partnership, conferring a privileged position and confirming their willingness to deepening contacts.

Although not institutionalised, it constitutes a first step towards the realisation of the material partnership, which, in favourable circumstances, can become real in the future. It can, therefore, be concluded that there is a mutual willingness for deepening the relationship and progressively fulfilling the content of the strategic Partnership Declaration.

The future of Polish-Mexican relations

Assuming that the priorities of Poland's foreign policy focus primarily on matters concerning Europe and Poland's immediate vicinity, it seems likely that, in the near future, there will be no breakthrough in Poland's relations with Latin America; direct contacts there will probably remain healthy, but not intensive – and this applies to Mexico as well. In the long term, however, a failure to address the need to intensify relations beyond Europe may lead to Poland becoming marginalised at the global level.

There is a need for a new, ambitious vision that lays out the global dimension of Polish foreign policy. Poland's view of the world must take account of the growing political importance and large economic potential of countries in the South, which are gradually becoming a focal point in international politics. In order to make effective use of its limited resources, a new strategy should focus on selected markets and regional centres, and must propose a practical set of political, economic and cultural instruments for increasing Poland's presence in those countries. The selection of strategic partners should be based on a country's potential, existing relation, and the role it plays in its region.

In a certain sense, Poland's relations with Mexico are an attempt to implement that plan; Poland treats Mexico as a priority trade partner outside Europe, and as a political ally. Its recognition of Mexico as a priority country within Latin America and the Caribbean may be seen as the first step in that direction – for the selection of the most important and most promising regional partners makes it possible to draw on their potential to the maximum and to overcome negative tendencies in the development of bilateral relations.

Polish-Mexican relations, despite a noticeable intensification in the last two decades, continue to stand at a low level of institutionalisation, even when compared with Poland's relations with other Latin American states. Trade relations are developing gradually, but feature a negative trade balance for Poland. And cultural relations, despite having achieved many successes in building up a positive image of the two states and in establishing positive social relations, are still not achieving their full potential. Polonia in Mexico, in turn, has not been considered in the Polonia policy of the government as an important focal point, and to a large extent is still left to its own devices. This is seen in the long-standing marginalisation of Mexico in Polish foreign policy and in the largely superficial character of bilateral relations, which must be fleshed out with real content at many levels.

In the opinion of analysts (Kugiel 2015: 2), there is a need to work out a long-term strategy towards non-European countries, including Mexico, and such a strategy should guarantee conditions for strengthening the political dialogue, economic cooperation, developmental aid and the promotion of culture. One can foresee within it outlays for intensifying interpersonal contacts by supporting visits by parliamentarians, scientists, members of civil society, etc. It would also be worth utilising the potential of the Polish diaspora and graduates of Polish universities in order to reinforce relations. While Poland's global interests mainly concern economic issues, a long-term strategy should also grant a greater role to political contacts, both bilateral and multilateral. Poland could then become more involved in forming EU policy towards priority countries (e.g. within the scope of free trade agreements or strategic partnerships), increasing its value as a partner, since up to now its level of activity within this scope has been insufficient. One can assume, therefore, that the European Union will continue to play a key role in increasing the significance of Latin America in Polish foreign policy (Wojna 2006: 64–65).

In order to transform the rhetorical motto of strategic partnership into reality, the willingness of the countries concerned is primarily needed. In full awareness of the existing restrictions and different priorities, it appears that both countries are currently closest to this assumption. In recent years, Mexico has become an important reference point of Polish foreign policy in the Latin American region, both as a political partner, as it was seen f.i. in the UN or the OECD, as well as economic, as a member of the dynamically developing PA. The first attempt at the broader institutionalisation of bilateral cooperation became a document created in 2016, "Recommendations for strengthening the relationship between Poland and Mexico", addressing the need to strengthen relations at the political level, business, and academic. During the first official visit of the Polish president in Mexico in 2017, a joint declaration was signed announcing a strategic partnership as well as twelve additional agreements, which should implement it in practice. One of the first steps to deepening the relationship became f.i. opening of the offices of military attachés – Polish in Mexico and Mexican in Warsaw.

In the context of Poland's relations with Mexico – a priority economic partner of Poland in Latin America and the Caribbean and a strategic partner – the most important challenge today remains how to implement the main postulates of the declared partnership, and how to add substance to the framework of positive relations created over many years by means of effective cooperation.

The 90th anniversary in 2018 of the establishment of Polish-Mexican diplomatic relations was a good moment to reflect on the future of the two states' bilateral relations. As announced in the joint communiqué signed on that occasion by the Ministries of Foreign Affairs of Poland and Mexico: "both states recognise that a tightening of economic and academic relations and cooperation will lead in the short term Mexico becoming a strategic partner of Poland in Latin America, and to Poland becoming a strategic partner of Mexico in Central Europe" (Joint Communiqué of the Ministry of Foreign Affairs of the Republic of Poland and the Ministry of Foreign Affairs of Mexico 2018: 2). There is hope, then, that the partnership will not remain merely declarative, but will become reality, and that bilateral relations will develop not only in accordance with accepted standards of cooperation, but also out of the conviction of both states that there is a need to invest them with deeper content.

Annex 1.

List of official visits

Heads of state/government	
1963	State visit by Prime Minister Józef Cyrankiewicz to Mexico
1963	Official visit of President Adolfo López Mateos to Poland
1998	State visit by Prime Minister Jerzy Buzek to Mexico
2004	State visit by President Vicente Fox to Poland
2004	Meeting between Presidents Aleksander Kwaśniewski and Vicente Fox during the 3rd European Union – Latin America and the Caribbean Summit in Vienna
2008	Meeting between Prime Minister Donald Tusk and President Felipe Calderon during the 5th European Union – Latin America and the Caribbean Summit in Lima
2014	Meeting between Presidents Bronisław Komorowski and Enrique Peña Nieto during the 69th General Assembly of the United Nations
2017	State visit by President Andrzej Duda to Mexico

Ministers of Foreign Affairs	
2000	Visit by Rosario Green to Warsaw
2003	Visit by Włodzimierz Cimoszewicz to Mexico
2013	Meeting between Radosław Sikorski and José Antonio Meade Kuribreña on the occasion of the 1st UE-CELAC Summit in Santiago
2015	Visit by José Antonio Meade Kuribreña to Warsaw

2015	Meeting between Mexican Foreign Minister Claudio Ruiz Massieu and the former Polish Foreign Minister Grzegorz Schetyna on the occasion of the 70th General Assembly of the United Nations in New York

Source: own study based on Recomendaciones para el fortalecimiento de la relación entre México y Polonia, Secretaría de Relaciones Exteriores México, Instituto Matías Romero 2016, p. 44.

Annex 2.

List of diplomatic representatives at the head of the Polish embassy in Mexico

Heads of Polish diplomatic outlets in Mexico	
Consulate General of the Republic of Poland	
1928–1931	Zygmunt Merdinger (Consul General RP)
Legation of RP	
1929–1931	Tytus Filipowicz (based in Washington)
1931*	Zygmunt Merdinger (envoy RP) – from 1936 also accredited in Colombia and Venezuela
1936	Tadeusz Jarocki (chargé d'affaires)
1936	Mieczysław Marchlewski (chargé d'affaires) – also accredited in Haiti and Guatemala
1940	Mieczysław Marchlewski (envoy) – also accredited in the Dominican Republic, Honduras, Colombia, Costa Rica, Nicaragua and Panama
1942	Władysław Neuman (envoy) – also accredited in Guatemala, Honduras, Costa Rica, Nicaragua and Panama
1945	Zygmunt Merdinger (envoy)
Legation and Embassy of PPR	
1945–1949	Jan Drohojowski (envoy)
1952	Bolesław Jeleń (envoy)
1958	Mieczysław Włodarek (envoy)
1960–1961	Mieczysław Włodarek (ambassador)
1962	Aleksander Bekier (chargé d'affaires)
1962	Jerzy Grudziński (ambassador)
1966	Ryszard Majchrzak

1972	Mieczysław Grad (ambassador)
1975	Józef Klasa (ambassador)
1980	Włodzimierz Janiurek (ambassador)
1982	Zdzisław Szewczyk (ambassador)
1985	Andrzej Załucki (chargé d'affaires)
1985	Henryk Łaszcz (ambassador) – also accredited in Costa Rica
Embassy of the Republic of Poland	
1989	Irena Gabor-Jatczak (ambassador)
1994	Joanna Kozińska-Frybes (ambassador)
1999	Przemysław Marzec (chargé d'affaires)
2000	Gabriel Beszłej (ambassador) – also accredited in Saint Lucia
2004	Wojciech Tomaszewski (ambassador) – also accredited in Saint Lucia
2007	Jacek Gawryszewski (chargé d'affaires)
2009	Anna Niewiadomska (ambassador) – also accredited in Belize, Guatemala, Honduras, Costa Rica, Nicaragua and El Salvador
2013	Beata Wojna (ambassador) also accredited in Belize, Guatemala, Honduras, Costa Rica, Nicaragua and El Salvador
2018	Paweł Woźny (chargé d'affaires)
2018	Maciej Ziętara (ambassador) – also accredited in Costa Rica
* date of nomination or accreditation	

Source: own study based on Krzysztof Smolana, Smolana Krzysztof, 2018, Polska i Meksyk na przestrzeni dziejów widziane z perspektywy misji dyplomatycznej, Meksyk, [online] Available at: <https://issuu.com/embajadadepoloniaenmexico/docs/polonia-me_xico-final_web> [accessed 30 July 2018], p. 357–358

Annex 3.

Joint declaration

"Towards a strategic partnership between Poland and Mexico"

1. At the invitation of the President of the United States of Mexico, Enrique Peña Nieto, the President of the Republic of Poland, Andrzej Duda, paid a state visit to Mexico on 22–25 April 2017.
2. The presidents recalled that Poland and Mexico established diplomatic relations in 1928, and emphasised the close, friendly character of those relations. Poland recalled Mexico's magnanimous acceptance during the World War II of Polish refugees, who settled in Santa Rosa in the State of Guanajuato.
3. Poland and Mexico confirmed their commitment to democratic values and human rights, and their joint will to build a world based on the principles of equality, social responsibility and security.
4. The Presidents acknowledged that Mexico's position in the western hemisphere, and Poland's role in the European Union and Central and Eastern Europe, increase opportunities to develop bilateral, regional and multilateral cooperation.
5. The presidents expressed their commitment to further strengthen bilateral relations by negotiating agreements that favour political, economic, cultural, scientific, educational, sports and police cooperation, and that ensure synergy in all areas of cooperation.

POLITICAL DIALOGUE

6. The Heads of State expressed their will to create a solid foundation for building stronger, more multi-dimensional relations between Poland and Mexico.
7. The Presidents emphasised the significance of maintaining a regular political dialogue at a high level as an instrument that facilitates cooperation and is conducive to making further bilateral commitments.
8. The Presidents agreed that they will maintain a substantive dialogue on regional and global issues by means of political and economic consultations. They reaffirmed their commitment to hold regular bilateral meetings within the framework of their mutual efforts to enhance the level of relations between Poland and Mexico in all aspects and to increase the significance of bilateral exchanges.
9. Poland expressed its support for the process of modernisation within the legal framework of cooperation between Mexico and the European Union, and emphasised that the results thereof are conducive to further intensifying collaboration beneficial to both parties.

10. Presidents Duda and Peña Nieto emphasised the contribution of parliamentary diplomacy in enriching bilateral relations and furthering mutual understanding between the two societies.

11. The parties agreed that they will increase the coordination of activities within multilateral organisations such as the UN and the OECD in areas of common interest including: human rights, UN reform, peacekeeping operations, disarmament and non-proliferation of weapons of mass destruction, sustainable development and climate change, and that they will implement joint analytical projects concerning Central America and the Caribbean.

12. The parties agreed that they will conduct a dialogue on matters concerning priority candidacies they may have in multilateral institutions. In this regard, Poland thanked Mexico for its support of its candidacy as a non-permanent member of the UN Security Council during the 2018–2019 term.

BILATERAL TRADE AND INVESTMENTS

13. The Presidents acknowledged that strengthening economic ties between Poland and Mexico is of key importance to the further development of their bilateral relations. They emphasised their conviction that free trade is a fundamental instrument for enabling economies to ensure greater employment opportunities, modernise their technologies and increase their export opportunities.

14. The parties emphasised the significance of the Global Agreement between Mexico and the EU for growth in their trade exchange.

15. Presidents Andrzej Duda and Peña Nieto welcomed the signing of the Declaration on Mutual Cooperation between the Ministry of Development and Finance of the Republic of Poland and the Ministry of Economy of Mexico for the purpose of creating a High Level Working Party for Economic Matters, which will be chaired by vice ministers.

16. As part of their engagement in promoting cooperation among the business communities of the two countries, the parties welcomed the signing of understandings between the Polish Bank Gospodarstwa Krajowego (BGK), Bancomext and the National Foreign Trade Bank of Mexico, and between the Polish Export Credit Insurance Corporation (KUKE) and Bancomext, the purposes of which are to promote bilateral trade and investment flow and to open in Mexico a Trade Office of the Polish Investment and Trade Agency.

17. The Presidents emphasised the significance of strengthening ties between the private sectors of both states in order to promote the creation of strategic business partnerships and more effective development of investment enterprises.

18. President Duda pointed out that Poland considers Mexico to be a pro-European market of high priority. In this context, the two Presidents agreed that they will continue to encourage Polish and Mexican entrepreneurs to take part in fairs and exhibitions organised in Mexico and Poland, respectively, as well as in trade missions, and will support such participation.

COOPERATION ON EDUCATION, CULTURE AND TECHNOLOGY

19. The Presidents emphasised the significance of cooperation on education, culture, sports, science and technology as a basis for promoting mutual understanding between the two countries, and as a valuable source of benefits for their societies.

20. In order to commemorate the 90th anniversary in 2018 of the establishment of diplomatic relations between them, Poland and Mexico agreed that they will conduct promotional activities aimed at encouraging their people to learn about the history and culture of the other country. Moreover, the organisation of a Conference of Rectors in Warsaw is foreseen.

21. The Heads of State welcomed the signing of the 4th Executive Programme to the Agreement on Cooperation in the Field of Education and Culture between Poland and Mexico, pursuant to which the two states engage in join activities in such fields as: higher education and cooperation between universities and other institutions; mobile learning; student exchanges; visits by youth leaders; the creation of study centres on Poland and Mexico at universities in both countries; language education; translations of literature; archeology; management of archives; and music, theatre and cinema.

22. In the conviction that young people are the main driving force behind sustainable development in both countries, the Presidents confirmed their support for: cooperation among universities; exchanges of students and teachers; scholarships; and activities aimed at facilitating and strengthening the implementation of scientific and education projects.

23. The Presidents acknowledged that sport and tourism are important tools for developing contacts among people and promoting cultural awareness in the relations between the two countries. They also agreed that they will encourage activities aimed at increasing tourism in both directions, and will cooperate within this scope.

24. The Presidents welcomed the confirmation that Mexico will be a partner country of the 2017 World Travel Show, the most important tourism fair in Poland, to be held at PTAK Warsaw Expo. This is a wonderful opportunity for Mexico to present its wide range of travel destinations and products.

25. Given that a large number of both Poles and Mexicans live abroad, the parties emphasised the importance of relations with their diasporas, and agreed that they will share experience within the scope of best practices in this area. Moreover, the parties committed themselves to promoting the perception of migrants as a source and driving force of development, both in the migrant target destination and in the place of origin, and to developing activities aimed at preventing discrimination while at the same time recognising the challenges and opportunities created by international migration.

26. The parties welcomed the signing during the state visit of the following acts of law:
   - The Fourth Executive Programme to the Agreement on cooperation in the field of education and culture between the Government of the Republic of Poland and the Government of the United States of Mexico for the years 2017–2021;
   - An Understanding on partnership between PTAK WARSAW EXPO and the Mexican Tourism Promotion Board in connection with the World Travel Show 2017 International travel show;
   - A Declaration on mutual cooperation between the Minister of Development and Finance of the Republic of Poland and the Ministry of Economy of the United States of Mexico;
   - A memorandum of understanding in the area of export credits between Bank Gospodarstwa Krajowego (BGK) and the Mexican National Credit Society (Bancomext);
   - A letter of intent between the Minister of Internal Affairs and Administration of the Republic of Poland and the Ministry of Administration of the United States of Mexico on Cooperation within the scope of training for police and border services;
   - An Agreement between the Minister of Sport and Tourism of the Republic of Poland and the National Commission for Physical Culture and Sport of the United States of Mexico on cooperation in the area of sport;
   - An agreement between the Polish Space Agency (POLSA) and the Mexican Space Agency (Agencia Espacial Mexican, AEM) on technical

and scientific cooperation within the scope of space research and the use of outer space for peaceful purposes;

- A memorandum of understanding between the PAIH and the Mexican agency for promoting trade and investment, ProMéxico;
- A memorandum of understanding on cooperation and information exchange between the Polish Press Agency (PAP) and the Mexican State Press Agency, Notimex;
- A cooperation agreement between the Polish National Chamber of Commerce (KIG) and the Mexican Council for Foreign Trade, Investments and Technology (COMCE).

27. The President of the Republic of Poland, Andrzej Duda, invited the President of the United States of Mexico, Enrique Peña Nieto, to pay a visit to Poland in order to further reinforce the friendly ties between their two countries. President Peña Nieto accepted the invitation with satisfaction. The date of the visit will be established through diplomatic channels.

28. This declaration was signed in Mexico City on the 24th of April 2017, in two original counterparts, one in the Polish language and one in the Spanish language, where the two language versions are of equal force.

Andrzej Duda

Prezydent
Rzeczypospolitej Polskiej

Enrique Peña Nieto

Prezydent
Meksykańskich Stanów Zjednoczonych

List of tables

Bibliography

Documents, legal acts

Central Statistical Office, 2015, Struktura narodowo-etniczna, językowa i wyznaniowa ludności Polski. National Population and Housing Census 2011, Warsaw

Constitution of the Republic of Poland of 2 April 1997, Journal of Laws of 1997 No. 78 item 483

Declaración Conjunta "Hacia una relación estratégica entre México y Polonia", 2017, [online] Available at: https://www.gob.mx/presidencia/documentos/declaracion-conjunta-hacia-una-relacion-estrategica-entre-mexico-y-polonia, [accessed 19 July 2018]

Exposé of Prime Minister Tadeusz Mazowiecki, 2001, [in]: Leszczyński Z., Kosecki A. (eds.), Stosunki międzynarodowe, dokumenty i materiały 1989–2002, Pułtusk

Hinz Krzysztof Jacek, 2015, Wyzwania dla polityki zagranicznej RP wobec Ameryki Łacińskiej i Karaibów (2015–2020 i po 2020), Warsaw

Leszczyński Zbigniew, Kosecki Adam (eds.), Stosunki międzynarodowe. Dokumenty i materiały 1989–2000, Wydawnictwo Wyższej Szkoły Humanistycznej w Pułtusku, Pułtusk 2001, p. 12–14.

Ministry of Foreign Affairs of the Republic of Poland, 2004, Strategia RP w odniesieniu do pozaeuropejskich krajów rozwijających się, Warsaw

Ministry of Foreign Affairs of the Republic of Poland, 2015, Rządowy program współpracy z Polonią i Polakami za granicą w latach 2015–2020, Warsaw

Ministry of Foreign Affairs of the Republic of Poland, 2016, "Recommendations on a strengthening of relations between Poland and Mexico": Ministry of Foreign Affairs of the Republic of Poland, Instituto Matías Romero

Ministry of Foreign Affairs of the Republic of Poland, 2018, Stosunki gospodarcze Polski z Meksykiem i Ameryką Środkową, [online] Available at: https://meksyk.msz.gov.pl/pl/wspolpraca_dwustronna/ekonomia/ambasada_rp_w_meksyku_340/ [accessed 18 July 2018]

Ministry of Foreign Affairs of the Republic of Poland, Minister Jacek Czaputowicz o priorytetach polskiej dyplomacji w 2018 roku – pełny tekst wystąpienia, [online] Available at: <https://www.euractiv.pl/section/polityka-zagraniczna/news/minister-jacek-czaputowicz-o-priorytetach-polskiej-dyplomacji-w-2018-roku-pelny-tekst-wystapienia/> [accessed 18 July 2018]

Ministry of Foreign Affairs of the Republic of Poland, Minister Witold
    Waszczykowski o priorytetach polskiej dyplomacji w 2017 roku, [online]
    Available at: <https://mfa.gov.pl/pl/aktualnosci/wiadomosci/minister_witold_
    waszczykowski_o_priorytetach_polskiej_dyplomacji > [accessed 18 July 2018]

Ministry of Foreign Affairs of the Republic of Poland, Minister Witold
    Waszczykowski o priorytetach polskiej dyplomacji w 2016 roku, [online]
    Available at: <https://mfa.gov.pl/pl/aktualnosci/wiadomosci/minister_witold_
    waszczykowski_o_priorytetach_polskiej_dyplomacji > [accessed 18 July 2018]

Ministry of Foreign Affairs of the Republic of Poland, Priorytety polskiej polityki
    zagranicznej 2012–2016, [online] Available at: https://www.premier.gov.pl/
    wydarzenia/decyzje-rzadu/priorytety-polskiej-polityki-zagranicznej-2012-
    2016-przedlozone-przez.html [accessed 30 July 2018]

Ministry of Foreign Affairs of the Republic of Poland, Secretaría de Relaciones
    Exteriores México, 2015, Zalecenia dotyczące wzmocnienia relacji między
    Polską a Meksykiem, Available at: < https://meksyk.msz.gov.pl/resource/
    dad85197-b3f8-4a09-aafa-2466b2a1f2cf:JCR>, [accessed 30 July 2018]

Ministry of Foreign Affairs of the Republic of Poland, Strategia Polskiej Polityki
    zagranicznej 2017–2021, [online] Available at: https://www.msz.gov.pl/
    resource/978285e3-5684-4fcb-8d7e-d0a8bfdb0fdb:JCR [accessed 30 July 218]

Ministry of Foreign Affairs of the Republic of Poland, 2019, Informacja Ministra
    Spraw Zagranicznych o zadaniach polskiej polityki zagranicznej w 2019 roku
    [online] Available https://www.gov.pl/web/dyplomacja/informacja-ministra-
    spraw-zagranicznych-o-zadaniach-polskiej-polityki-zagranicznej-w-2019-
    roku [accessed 20 November 2019]

Ministry of Foreign Affairs of the Republic of Poland, Consular Department,
    2016, Raport polskiej służby dyplomatyczno-konsularnej za 2015 rok, Warsaw

Parliament of the Republic of Poland, 7th term, Sprawozdanie stenograficzne
    z 91. posiedzenia Sejmu Rzeczypospolitej Polskiej w dniu 23 kwietnia 2015,
    2015, Informacja ministra spraw zagranicznych Polski, Grzegorza Schetyny,
    o zadaniach polskiej polityki zagranicznej w 2015 roku. [pdf] available at
    <orka2.sejm.gov.pl/StenoInter7.nsf/0/07D5239CA45617BCC1257E31000FA5
    9E/%24File/91_b_ksiazka_bis.pdf> [accessed 30 July 2018]

Strategia na rzecz odpowiedzialnego rozwoju do roku 2020 (z perspektywą do
    2030 r.), 2017, [pdf] Available at: <https://www.miir.gov.pl/media/48672/
    SOR.pdf> [accessed 28 June 2018]

Umowa o współpracy w dziedzinie edukacji i kultury między Rządem
    Rzeczypospolitej Polskiej a Rządem Meksykańskich Stanów Zjednoczonych,
    sporządzona w Warszawie dnia 12 czerwca 1997 r., Dziennik Ustaw nr 54,
    poz. 344, 1998

Ustawa z dnia 4 września 1997 r. o działach administracji rządowej, Journal of
    Laws of 1997 No. 141 item 943

Memoirs

Słabczyński Wacław, 1957, Paweł Edmund Strzelecki. Podróże-Odkrycia-Prace, Warsaw: Polish Scientific Publishers PWN

Books and monographs

Burant Stephen, 2000, Stosunki polsko-ukraińskie a idea strategicznego partnerstwa, Warszawa

Dobosiewicz Zbigniew, Rómmel Waldemar (eds.), 1977, Polonia w Ameryce Łacińskiej, Lublin: Lublin Press

Lerski Jerzy J., 1958, A Polish Chapter in Jacksonian America: The United States and Polish exiles of 1831, Madison

Łepkowski Tadeusz, 1980, Polska-Meksyk 1918–1939, Wrocław: Ossolineum Press

Paradowska Maria, 1985, Polacy w Meksyku i Ameryce Środkowej, Wrocław; Zakład Narodowy im. Ossolińskich.

Pi-Suñer Antonia, Riguzzi Paolo, Ruano Lorena, 2011, Historia de las relaciones internacionales de México, 1821–2010, Europa, vol. 5, México: Secretaría de las Relaciones Exteriores de México

Smolana Krzysztof, 2018, Polska i Meksyk na przestrzeni dziejów widziane z perspektywy misji dyplomatycznej, Meksyk, [online] Available at: <https://issuu.com/embajadadepoloniaenmexico/docs/polonia-me_xico-final_web> [accessed 30 July 2018]

Zając Justyna, Zięba Ryszard, 2005, Polska w stosunkach międzynarodowych 1945–1989. Toruń: Adam Marszałek Press

Zięba Ryszard, 2010, Główne kierunki polityki zagranicznej Polski po zimnej wojnie, Warsaw: Academic and Professional Press

Papers

Bałon Krzysztof, 2001, Co to jest partnerstwo strategiczne?, "Biuletyn", Polski Instytut Spraw Międzynarodowych, nr 34

Bogdziewicz Paweł, 2002, Stosunki dwustronne Polski. Meksyk, "Rocznik Polskiej Polityki Zagranicznej"

de Icaza Carlos, 2018, México y Europa: una historia de amistad, solidaridad, y cooperación, "Revista Mexicana de Política Exterior", enero-abril de 2018, núm. 112

Demechu Degefe, 2006, Stosunki polsko-etiopskie. Zarys problematyki, "Forum Politologiczne", vol. 3

Dumała Hanna, 1997, Polska-Ameryka Łacińska. Powojenne stosunki dyplomatyczno-konsularne, "Annales Universitatis Mariae Curie-Skłodowska Lublin Polonia", vol. IV

Gawrycki Marcin F., 2010, Polityka Polski wobec państw Ameryki Łacińskiej, [in]: Stanisław Bieleń (ed.), Polityka zagraniczna Polski po wstąpieniu do NATO i UE. Problemy tożsamości i adaptacji, Warsaw: Difin

Gocłowska-Bolek Joanna, 2009, Obecność Ameryki Łacińskiej w polskiej gospodarce i wymianie handlowej, [in]: Andrzej Dembicz (ed.), Ameryka Łacińska w polskiej polityce, Warsaw: CESLA UW

Jacorzynski Witold Robert, Kozlowski Marcin Jacek, 2015, Rostros de la presencia polaca en México: un vuelo a través de la historia, Ulúa. Revista de Historia, Sociedad, Cultura, julio-diciembre, nr 26

Kacperczyk Katarzyna, 2005, Polska polityka zagraniczna w świetle Strategii RP w odniesieniu do pozaeuropejskich krajów rozwijających się, "Rocznik Polskiej Polityki Zagranicznej"

Kugiel Patryk, 2015, Go Global: nowa strategia współpracy z krajami rozwijającymi się, "Biuletyn PISM", Polski Instytut Stosunków Międzynarodowych, 17 (1244)

Latin American and Caribbean Team, Department of America, Ministry of Foreign Affairs of the Republic of Poland, 2009, Stosunki Polska – Ameryka Łacińska i Karaiby, [in]: Dembicz Andrzej (ed.), Ameryka Łacińska w polskiej polityce, Warsaw: CESLA UW

Lizak Wiesław, Spyra Jarosław, 2002, Azja, Bliski Wschód i Ameryka Łacińska w polityce zagranicznej RP, [in]: Roman Kuźniar, Krzysztof Szczepanik (eds.), Polityka zagraniczna RP 1989–2002, Warsaw: Askon Press

Łepkowski Tadeusz, 1970, Z dziejów kontaktów polsko-meksykańskich w XIX i XX w., "Etnografia Polska", XIV (2)

Miodek Lech, 2009, Obecność Ameryki Łacińskiej w polskiej polityce zagranicznej – przegląd stosunków wzajemnych w latach 1990–2005, [in]: Dembicz Andrzej (ed.), Ameryka Łacińska w polskiej polityce, Warsaw: "Dokumenty Robocze CESLA"

Moloeznik Marcos Pablo, 2007, Stosunki dyplomatyczne polsko-meksykańskie z perspektywy historycznej, [in]: Villagómez Porras Fernando (ed.), Relacje Polska-Meksyk. Historia i współczesność, Warsaw: CESLA

Oberda Monkiewicz Anita, 2016, Meksyk – mocarstwo niechętne?, [in]: Marcin F. Gawrycki, Edward Haliżak, Roman Kuźniar, Michałowska Grażyna, Popławki Dariusz, Zajączkowski Jakub, Zięba Ryszard (eds.), Tendencje i procesy rozwojowe współczesnych stosunków międzynarodowych, Warsaw: Scholar Academic Press

Olejniczak Dorota K., 2007, Społeczność polska w Meksyku, [in]: Villagómez Porras Fernando (ed.), Relacje Polska-Meksyk. Historia i współczesność, Warsaw: CESLA UW

Osińska Lucyna, Polskie a ukraińskie pojmowanie partnerstwa strategicznego pomiędzy Warszawą a Kijowem, "Dialogi polityczne", 2007, nr 8

Rudowski Tomasz, 2014, Polska polityka wobec Ameryki Łacińskiej, [in]: Adam Dąbrowski, Ludwiniak Mateusz (eds.), Nowe spojrzenia w naukach o polityce, vol. 5, Warsaw

Rycerz Danuta, 2007, Polsko-meksykańskie kontakty kulturalne, [in]: Villagómez Porras Fernando (ed.), Relacje Polska-Meksyk. Historia i współczesność, Warsaw: CESLA UW

Rynkowska Marta, 2007, Rola dyplomacji parlamentarnej w kontekście polsko-meksykańskich stosunków parlamentarnych, [in]: Villagómez Porras Fernando (ed.), Relacje Polska-Meksyk. Historia i współczesność, Warsaw: CESLA

Smyk Radosław, Grudziński Adam, 2007, Stosunki gospodarcze Meksyk-Polska, [in]: Villagómez Porras Fernando (ed.), Relacje Polska-Meksyk. Historia i współczesność, Warsaw: CESLA UW

Spyra Jarosław, 2006, Stosunki Polski z krajami Ameryki Łacińskiej, [in]: Gawrycki Marcin F. (ed.), Ameryka Łacińska we współczesnym świecie, Warsaw: Warsaw University Press

Stemplowski Ryszard, 2001, Następny krok w strategicznym partnerstwie polsko-litewskim, "Polski Przegląd Dyplomatyczny", nr 2 (1)

Wojna Beata, 2006, Polska polityka wobec Ameryki Łacińskiej i Karaibów – bilans możliwości rozwoju stosunków z perspektywy członkostwa w Unii Europejskiej Polski, "Przegląd Dyplomatyczny", nr 32 (4)

Żurawska Monika, 2014, Polsko-meksykańska wymiana handlowa w okresie prezydentury Carlosa Salinasa de Gortari oraz Vicente Foxa, [in]: Drgas Michał, Knopek Jacek, Ratke-Majewska Anna (eds.), Polska-Ameryka Łacińska. Historia-Polityka-Gospodarka-Kultura, Toruń: Adam Marszałek Press

Newspapers

Piwowarczyk Piotr, 2012, Meksykański dom polskich uchodźców. Uchodźcy z Santa Rosa, Polityka, 10 marca, [online] Available at: <https://www.polityka.pl/tygodnikpolityka/historia/1524695,1,meksykanski-dom-polskich-uchodzcow.read> [accessed 10 July 2018]

W Polityce, 24.04.2017, Na początek spotkanie z Polonią. Andrzej Duda odznaczył zasłużonych w działalności polonijnej w Meksyku, [online]

Available at: https://wpolityce.pl/spoleczenstwo/336834-na-poczatek-spotkanie-z-polonia-andrzej-duda-odznaczyl-zasluzonych-w-dzialalnosci-polonijnej-w-meksyku-zobacz-zdjecia [accessed 10 July 2018]

Websites

Alianza del Pacífico. El poder de la integración, 2018, [online] Available at: https://alianzapacifico.net/en/what-is-the-pacific-alliance/ [accessed 24 July 2018]

El poder de la integración, 2018, [online] Available at: http://amapolamexico. blogspot.com/p/dla-polakow.html [accessed 08 July 2018]

Fedoruk Aleksander, 2018, Meksyk bramą dla polskich towarów i inwestycji za oceanem, "Business Insider", [e-journal] Available through: https:// businessinsider.com.pl/firmy/strategie/wymiana-handlowa-polska-meksyk-inwestycje-w-meksyku/vk44c45 [accessed 27 June 2018]

Gazeta Prawna, 06.06.2018, Komisja pozytywnie o kandydatach na ambasadorów w Meksyku i Kostaryce oraz na Słowacji, [online] Available at: <www.gazetaprawna.pl> [accessed 30 July 2018]

Inauguran en el Senado exposición fotográfica "Polonia, un país de patrimonio mundial", 2017, Boletin, [online] Available at: http://comunicacion.senado. gob.mx/index.php/informacion/boletines/36063-inauguran-en-el-senado-exposicion-fotografica-polonia-un-pais-de-patrimonio-mundial.html>> [accessed 12 July 2018]

Informator ekonomiczny – Meksyk, Ministerstwo Spraw Zagranicznych RP, 2018, [online] Available at: <https://informatorekonomiczny.msz.gov.pl/pl/ ameryka_polnocna_i_srodkowa/meksyk/meksyk> [accessed 19 July 2018]

Komisja Europejska, Komunikat Prasowy, 21.04.2018, UE i Meksyk osiągnęły nowe porozumienie w sprawie handlu [pdf] Available at: <https://http:// webcache.googleusercontent.com/search?q=cache:6COHwz7erqIJ:europa. eu/rapid/press-release_IP-18-782_pl.pdf+&cd=3&hl=pl&ct=clnk&gl=pl>> [accessed 31 July 2018]

Mexico and Poland: Centuries of Cultural Relations, 2015, [online] Available at: <https://culture.pl/en/article/mexico-and-poland-centuries-of-cultural-relations> [accessed 26 July 2018]

Ministry of Development, 2017, Notatka n/t polsko-meksykańskiej współpracy gospodarczej, Departament Współpracy Międzynarodowej, [pdf] Available at: <https://www.mpit.gov.pl/media/39377/Meksyk_13_06_2017.pdf> [accessed 27 June 2018]

Ministry of Foreign Affairs of the Republic of Poland, 2014, Atlas polskiej obecności w świecie, Ministerstwo Spraw Zagranicznych, [online] Available

at: <https://www.msz.gov.pl/pl/polityka_zagraniczna/polonia/atlas_polskiej_
obecnosci_w_swiecie> [accessed 30 July 2018]

Ministry of Foreign Affairs of the Republic of Poland, "Sojusz Pacyfiku –
gospodarcze wyzwanie dla Polski", 2017, [online] Available at: <https://www.
msz.gov.pl/pl/p/msz_pl/polityka_zagraniczna/inne_kontynenty/ameryka_
lacinska_i_karaiby/sojusz_pacyfiku___gospodarcze_wyzwanie_dla_polski;js
essionid=BB592434CDDED528996EB97C81FC0209.cmsap6p> [accessed 19
July 2018]

Ministry of Foreign Affairs of the Republic of Poland, 2018, Polsko-
meksykańskie konsultacje polityczne [online] Available at: https://www.
msz.gov.pl/pl/aktualnosci/wiadomosci/polsko_meksykanskie_konsultacje_
polityczne>> [accessed 31 July 2018]

Ministry of Foreign Affairs of the Republic of Poland, 2018, Wspólny komunikat
MSZ RP i MSZ Meksyku, Polska i Meksyk obchodzą 90-lecie ustanowienia
stosunków międzypaństwowych. [online] Available at: https://www.msz.gov.
pl/resource/75eab87c-70be-4b67-8963-2ec1d36d7905:JCR [accessed 31 July
2018]

Ministry of Foreign Affairs of the Republic of Poland, Relacje Polski z krajami
Ameryki Łacińskiej i Karaibami, [online] at: https://www.msz.gov.pl/pl/
polityka_zagraniczna/inne_kontynenty/ameryka_lacinska_i_karaiby/
stosunki_dwustronne_ameryka_lacinska_karaiby/stosunki_polska___
ameryka_lacinska_i_karaiby [accessed 15 July 2018]

Ministry of Science and Higher Education, Polska zacieśnia współpracę z
Meksykiem, [online] Available at: https://www.nauka.gov.pl/ministerstwo/
wspolpraca-z-zagranica/wspolpraca-dwustronna/mapa-swiata/meksyk/
polska-zaciesnia-wspolprace-z-meksykiem.html [accessed 30 July 2018]

Index of names

Studies in Politics, Security and Society

Edited by Stanisław Sulowski

www.peterlang.com